SOUNDS AND SINS OF SINGLISH
AND OTHER NONSENSE

REX SHELLEY
BENG KIA-SU
TAKUT BIN SALAH

TIMES BOOKS INTERNATIONAL
Kuala Lumpur • Singapore

Illustrations on pages 29, 37, 62, 68, 77, 82,
85, 107, 121, 125, 147 (second), 148, 173
by Shirley Eu-Wong
All other illustrations by Rex Shelley

© 1995 Times Editions Pte Ltd
© 2000 Times Media Private Limited

Published by Times Books International
An imprint of Times Media Private Limited
A member of the Times Publishing Group
Times Centre, 1 New Industrial Road, Singapore 536196
Tel: (65) 2848844 Fax: (65) 2854871
Email: te@tpl.com.sg
Online bookstore: http://www.timesone.com.sg/te

Times Subang
Lot 46, Subang Hi-Tech Industrial Park
Batu Tiga, 40000 Shah Alam
Selangor Darul Ehsan, Malaysia
Tel & Fax: (603) 7363517
Email: cchong@tpg.com.my

All rights reserved. No part of this publication may be
reproduced, stored in a retrieval system, or transmitted,
in any form or by any means, electronic, mechanical,
photocopying, recording or otherwise, without the prior
permission of the copyright owner.

Printed in Singapore

ISBN 981 204 392 6

"Improving the proficiency of English is the most important task. I make no apologies for this emphasis. Singapore is an international city."

—Minister of Education (*Straits Times*, 4 February 1985)

FREE CHIA THYE POH!

— with every $20.- of purchases

late is late oraidy

Mr Loo is a shithouse!
— Mr WC. Loo?

Don't vote!

Ah Kow luves mimi — allatime?

mimi is a fraud!

GIMME GUM!

My marder made me a schizophrenic

If I gave her the wool, would she knit one for m...

no smirking

Foreword

This book is about the unique form of the English language that is spoken and written in Singapore, often referred to as Singlish. People talk of this variety of the English language but no one has defined Singlish as yet. So we have collected together some deviations from generally accepted forms of English and present a mixed bag of Singlish.

We wrote this book both for people who come to Singapore and have to deal with Singaporeans and for our own people so that they can see the differences in their speech and writing which puzzle, confuse and often amuse visitors from other English-speaking countries.

It is our hope that some of our teachers may benefit from our Singlish collection; but we would have much misgiving if they use our rough and ready book as a reference because they need something more than what we present here. We have not written a book which has sufficient width or depth for them. Our collection only skims along the surface with wild comments and frivolity that make it readable lying on a beach or bed.

Reference bases had to be found for this book because Singlish is an amorphous body of deviations from Standard English; and Standard English is something equally woolly, vague and lumpy. So we have taken what the world now describes as RP (the old BBC English) as our pronunciation reference.

English grammar does not pose any major problems of a reference benchmark. It is fairly clear and structured. There are very few spelling controversies, and we have related Singlish to both the American and British versions of grammar and vocabulary.

We tried not to make judgements on what is right or wrong but personal prejudices kept creeping in. Sorry, lah!

The correct form or pronunciation was given here and there. Readers who really want to improve their Singlish must make a habit of looking up the dictionary.

We have thrown in a lot of irreverent comments and notes on other varieties of English and made many diversions, but we hope all this junk will bring to the reader an awareness that language is important. We admit our rather light-hearted approach to the whole thing because we have set out to prod and amuse and thereby sneak in a little education.

Rex Shelley, Beng Kia-Su and Takut bin Salah
(My co-authors decided to use pen-names just in case the book is a failure and I agreed to this with alacrity as I have two readily available anonymous Singlish 'scrapegoats'. —Rex Shelley.)

A

a The first sin of Singlish in alphabetical sequence is a sin of omission. The article or determinant *a* or *an* is very often dropped.

Crewe in his book on Singapore English (ref. 5) gives some examples of the sin of omission:
Much of the meat I bought is rotten but at least few pieces are still edible.
Currently I am working as quantity surveyor.

Even an official notice omitted the article:
Have you displayed parking coupon?

There is the equally common error of pushing in an 'a' when there is no need to have one; what we call the sin of redundancy: *I have implemented it on a hardware.*

abacus It must be a daunting thought to English teachers that the first useful word in the dictionary, after rarely encountered words like *aardvark*, is given a Singlish pronunciation twist. Singlish speakers put the accent on the second syllable. A real fear runs right through Singlish users of pronouncing words with an accent on the first syllable. In the case of *abacus*, the Singlish pronunciation gives it overtones of the towkay working on his beads and thinking of the profits and all the XO brandy they will bring. It sounds like *a Bacchus*, the Greek God of wine and what-have-you in the way of alcohol, whose birthday, December 25th, seems to be celebrated with gusto in Singapore. Surely it must be *his* day and not the other one which non-Christians, and perhaps even some Christians honour with liberal litres of liquor.

Other examples of Singlish putting the accent on the second syllable and not on the first as it should be are *carpenter, interesting*.

Abestos, air-bestos, asbestos For some reason almost everyone in Singapore drops the first *s* in *asbestos*. We know it is a dirty word in greenie circles but there is no need to mutilate it with a mute *s*.

abourrt A unique sound. An *r* is introduced into *about*. It is slurred and rolled around the mouth. It sounds like, but is not quite, the American drawled *r*. A variation is *abourritt*; about it. And a whole train of slurring occurs in *howbourit*.

abovementioned Not wrong, but archaic and still used by civil servants. Letters need headings to forewarn the reader of the subject. But having headed your letter with the appropriate title there is no earthly need to say it's there on top. It has done its job and can fade away nicely.

abzurd An example of what someone called 'zedding the ess'. The *s* sound of *ab-serd* becomes a *z* sound in Singlish. It is a very common sin of Singlish. But the *z* sound is not really overworked in Singlish because Singlish takes a very balanced approach to the matter and the complimentary fault of 'essing the zed' occurs with equal frequency. The books balance nicely.

Examples of 'zedding the ess': Dezember,

converzation, courzes, nurzery, choizes, embarrazzing, excurzion, bazed on. Examples of 'essing the zed': enthusiasm, essactly, plasma.

acronyms Singaporeans revel in creating what they call acronyms. To understand the real Singlish of the people one has to know the basic abbreviations of Singapore life.

Some of them used in this book are:

CBD	–	Central Beesness District
CPF	–	Central Proveedent Fund
HDB–		Housing and Devalopment Board
NPB	–	National Prodarctivity Board
NS	–	National Service (perfect in pronunciation)
NUS	–	National Unierrrrsity of Singapore
OUB	–	Owerseas Union Bank
PAP	–	Piple's Action Party
PUB	–	Parblic Utilities Board
SBC	–	Singapore Broatcasting Copperation
SDF	–	Starff Devalopment Fund

The word acronym has another meaning in Singlish. In good honest-to-God English, an acronym is when the initials of a phrase are used to make another word. Nato is an example. Scuba is another. It was coined from Small Compact Underwater Breathing Apparatus.

Using the alphabetical sounds of H and D and B does not make HDB an acronym. If you say Nus (pronounced *noose*) for NUS, on the other hand, you have an acronym. Government publications invariably make this error.

actsy Playing up, acting up, preening, peacock-prancing; a descriptive Singlish creation. Becoming obsolete?

adjective The Singlish way stresses the *jek* bit. Our dictionary says, ad'jek tive.

Does Singlish accept foreign words? See *allamak*.

adoll-essence The correct pronunciation has the accent on the *less* syllable, ad-o-les'ence; lesser than a full adult.

advance *Computer science is so advance nowadays. Advanced cash bookings.* Confusion of past and present tense. There is equal confusion of past and future tenses. Vehicle indicators in Singlish-Singapore do not say "I am going to change lanes" but "I have changed lanes." We spotted one odd use of the verb *to advance* in a coffee shop some years ago, Advance Popiah.

advertisement A common mispronunciation makes the penultimate syllable rhyme with the last syllable of hypnotise instead of rhyming with his or fizz; a subconscious slip? The accent is also misplaced on the wrong *tise* sound. Here we have a word with the accent on the second syllable which Singlish speakers seem to have a strong urge to do, and the opportunity is missed.

advise Very, very often used incorrectly in two ways: *He advice me that I should improve my grammar. Thank you for your advise that I should improve my grammar.*

Advice is the noun; one gives advice. *Advise* is the verb. One advises. If he advised you to improve your grammar we think you should thank him for his advice.

We give another example of the correct use of the word advice below.

It has been said there are two kinds of fools in the world; those who give advice and those who do not take it. I propose to belong to the first category in the hope that you will not belong to the second.
(N.A. Palkhivala)

aerobic *I do aerobic every day.* Maybe just one deep breath? No. There is no such singular exercise. There is no singular to *aerobics*.

The singular and plural are continuously used incorrectly in Singlish. Common errors are oversea, informations, science fictions, grammars, he wears spectacle, stars-spangled flag, all staffs should observe the laws and flush the toilet after using, aircrafts, scissor, trouser, plier, upstair.

aeroplane Quite often this sort of adjectival use of a noun is a stumbling block as in, *Have you got any aeroplanes books?* for *Have you got any aeroplane books?*

after *After* has been adapted in Singlish to compress the whole phrase, *If we do this then ...* into a single pithy word: *After people talk ...*

This is one of the basic characteristics of Singlish: economy of words and sounds. Whole phrases are telescoped into a single new word creation or compressed orally into a single grunt. Multi-syllable words are collapsed into shorter barely intelligible mumbles. Maybe it reflects a laudable streak in Singaporeans to get on with it and not waste time and breath unnecessarily. Or a propensity to cut corners?

That old song, *People Will Say We're In Love* could be bombed with the Singlish ending.

> Don't throw bouquets at me,
> Don't please my folks too much,
> Don't laugh at my jokes too much ...
> After people talk ...

Apart from telescoping phrases, Singlish compresses words, throwing out syllables it considers unnecessary.

Again? Say again? This word or phrase, which means *I beg your pardon*, has come into general use in recent years. We believe it originates from National Service in the Armed Forces where *say again* is the preferred phrase for *pardon*, or *please repeat* as it is very clear in walkie-talkie chatter.

Sometimes pronounced *a-gain*. Often included unnecessarily. Examples from Tongue (ref. 21):
No need to return the cheque again. Repeat again!

Agatha Few Singaporeans realise that the name should be pronounced with the first *a* as in cat, sat, mat; the other two *a*'s as in infant or the last *a* of Australia. This is another example of shying away from accents on the first syllable.

age *We try to be in the leading age of technology.* We think he really meant *edge*. It would be nice and ambiguous if the mispronunciation occurred in this sentence: He has the *age* over us.

Ah Beng Every family or social group sooner or later creates a word for the simpleton. Singaporeans use *Ah Beng* as one such stooge. And from *Ah Beng*, phrases like Ah Beng pants, Ah Beng manners, gait, etc. are spun off.

ahh A sound that has much versatility in Singapore. It can be used in any part of a sentence or phrase to indicate shock, surprise, delight, sudden understanding, etc. When used after *thank you*, it does emphasise one's gratitude in a special charming Singapore way: *Tankyou ahh.* Ahh is also used as a suffix of intimacy, as in *Heng, ahh* ... Do not confuse the gentle friendly address of *Heng, ahh* ... with the run-of-the-mill nickname of Ah Heng. Once the fellow is called Ah Heng, anyone can call him that, but only at the right time and place can you use the tender *Ah Heng, ahh* ... The application is bisexual.

aigs Offered by some waiters as *flied aigs*. It is only because of this Singapore-Malaysian pronunciation that Mr Oh (ref. 12) could make his pun, *One hen to another, My ache has disappeared!* Singlish abhors the harsh sound of the *gger* in eggs.

aircon This is now a standard abbreviation all over the English-speaking world, but there is an occasional Singlish version, the *air-condition*. *What an old air-condition you have!* (Prospective tenant to landlord.)

airff The Singlish F. We hear it continuously on FM bands.

airmistrashun A common version of *administration*. A whole series of Singlish mispronunciations forgets about the *d* or *b* within a word.

airnergetic The Singlish for energetic. The *en* first syllable appears to take too much energy and in accordance with the Singlish principle of saving energy, an easy *air* sound is used.

Airwood Toh Paik Choo has finally found its original sound – Edward. A breakthrough in Singlish detection scholarship!

aiyah! Usually uttered with a gasp of surprise or exasperation. The Malay equivalent of *Oh dear!* Drawl the *yah* out and give it some punchy emphasis for better effect.

akk As in *The Land Acquisition Akk*, one of the millstones round our necks; it's the pronunciation we mean.

akseedent The *dent* is emphasised. A graphic error. The correct English version *ak'si-dent* (accent on *ac*) is seldom heard.

allamak A Malay ejaculation, similar to *Mama mia!* Occurs frequently in Singaporean conversation.

allainge The classic 'elling of the arr', as in the age-old Chinese dish of flied-lice, changes arrange to allainge.

allert While Singlish usually misses an alphabet in its drive for oral economy, with *alert*, it adds another *l* for good measure. Our dictionary reads, a-lert'. W.J. Crewe (ref. 5) touches on the importance of alertness in his introduction: *One will never improve one's Singlish if one is not alert to the differences in one's speech from RP (Received Pronunciation); in two directions: listening to one's own speech and to the speech of native English speakers.*

All-liver All-lever at times. The Singlish Oliver twist.

almeira An old Portuguese word for cupboard which sometimes crept into Singlish in the old days. An epistemological relic of the past.

along *Don't forget to bring along the umbrella.* An example of Singlish's occasional redundancy which counterbalances the more common omission of a word or letter.

also Like *after*, *also* sometimes represents a whole phrase. *The kwayteow at Cassia Crayscent is really top class, man ... laksa also good.*

The incorrect position of *also* is also a common error, as in *The line spacing also can be adjusted by command ^OS 1-9.*

alternatives The Singlish sound can at times be confused with *all der natives*. Our dictionary reads, awl-ter'-na-tiv.

aluminium Pronounced the American way at times although it is hardly ever spelt the American way (aluminum).

American pronunciation This varies across the USA, but John Honey (ref. 8) points out, "The American accent sounds noticeably different from RP (Received Pronunciation, the present-day paragon of oral English), yet apart from a handful of words like deTAIL, baTON, INquiry, LABoratory, AdverTISment and harASS ... the Americans put the stress on the same syllable of the word as the British do. The same is true of Australian, New Zealand and South African accents, and largely true of West Indian accents, though not of West and East African varieties."

anarder A parallel to *udder* (see **udder**). 'Anarder' Singlish pronunciation error.

anen-err A fairly common mumble to gain thinking time. It comes from ... *and then err* ...

> "I have travelled more than anyone else, and have noticed that even angels speak English with an accent." —Mark Twain

angkat To *angkat* someone is to curry favour with him. It comes from the Malay verb *to carry*. The detailed derivation is too crude for this G-rated book.

Annalai We asked a little boy what name he would like his new sister to have, and he answered without hesitation, "Annalai!" It turned out that this was his kindy teacher's name: Anna Lai. We wondered how many of those unusual names Singapore children are inflicted with originated in this fashion. Fifty years ago partially literate clerks at the Registry of Births and Deaths saddled many Singaporeans with unique names. And as the cinema brought a whole new perspective to both selecting names on the part of parents and spelling them on the part of Registry clerks these aberrations rose to a peak and gradually died away.

New offbeat trends slowly emerged. The name that was different began to hold a certain fascination for shortsighted parents.

We wonder whether these creations merit a place in a record of Singlish. Perhaps they do where new sounds are born. Names like Dainty and Honey do not contribute new sounds, but Essie (from Elsie?), Annalai, Carlyn (from Carl and Lynette, or maybe Carolyn) may add to the differences that make Singlish what it is; even though some of them bring new pronunciation problems.

Pancy is one such name. We also heard another on the air – Season, which she explained her father derived from the fact that she was a 'Caesarean' baby. And a bitter one, Quinine.

In one of Arnold Bennet's books, the mother of a character, Edward Henry, calls her son Denry. "She saved a certain amount of time every day by addressing her son as Denry, instead of Edward Henry."

> "Must a name mean something?" Alice asked doubtfully.
> "Of course it must," Humpty Dumpty said.

anonymous A rare gem of a verbal error which perhaps could recur. *The decision was anonymous, completely anonymous.*

append One sees *append* used in place of *listed*, or *set out* fairly frequently in business letters. *We append below the prices you requested.* To append is to add on. One can have a price-list appended to the letter, i.e., added on as a separate sheet – an appendix. But unless you have stapled below a scrappy bit of paper with the prices on it, the *append below* construction is incorrect. Use either *list below* or *set out below*.

appreciate One could interpret the common ending to a request in business letters that *We will appreciate if this can be carried out as soon as possible* kindly as an appeal to help increase the assets of the company. Singlish ignores the fact that *appreciate* needs an object. (It should be, "We will appreciate it if …")

Arlohdee This is a cornerstone sound of Singlish. It is Ah Beng's version of ROD, the date of being relieved from duty as a national serviceman, or NSman, invariably referred to as the *run-out-date*. (ROD has now been changed to ORD, a positive phrase, *operationally ready for duty*). It has been said that every mother's son in Singapore has his ROD engraved in his memory, often more deeply than his birthday. National Service has become an integral part of every male's life and of every mother of a male in Singapore. And it is a major element in toughening up the male Singaporean and ageing his mother. The experience of being a soldier is a hard and rich one. Rudyard Kipling expressed the lonely thoughts of the British soldier in the harsh bare hills of Afghanistan with his beautiful poem which starts with ...

> There's a rock to the left and a rock to the right,
> And a low lean thorn in between,
> And ye may hear a breechbolt snick,
> Where ne'er a man is seen.

Beng Kia-Su has written the Singlish version of this. But it is written in a subset of Singlish known as NS slang, and we have to lead you into his poem gently with a preamble of NS slang translations.

Blank = blur (Singlish)

Blerdy = bloody

Blur = dazed, dense, dizzy (Singlish)

Bobo King = a poor marksman (Singlish)

Brief = briefing (English)

Catch no ball = liak bo kiu in Hokkien, meaning that nothing was understood at the lecture or briefing

Cheng Hu = officers (Hokkien)

Chuak = frightened (Hokkien)

Debrief = debriefing (plain English)
FIBUA = fighting in built-up areas (*meeatary* English acronym)
Frus = frustrated (Singlish)
Gabra = panic, confusion (original language source unknown)
Havoc = to create havoc, trouble, disobey (English)
Helicopter = Chinese-educated soldier. The origin of this is reported to be the explanation a recruit gave for his poor English, *I am Chinese helucated.*)
Kena = to get, receive, catch it (Malay)
Khoon = sleep, sleepy (Hokkien)
Lecluit = See **arrah** below (Pidgin English)
Liam keng = to recite prayers in Hokkien, meaning the dreary repeating of instructions by some officers.
No hew = No interest, disregarding instructions (Hokkien)
Shag = dead beat, tired out (from the English)
Sin Chiau = new recruit (Hokkien)
Skive = tuang (English)
Soleed = solid, with the *i* drawn out. It means solid, intense, fierce, reliable (extended English)
Tuang = to run away from one's duty, hide (Malay?)
Upside-down screw = to be punished severely, painfully (distorted, contorted English)
Wake up = be attentive, be on the ball. The variant is *wake up your idea*, meaning *think, you idiot, think!* (English or Irish)

ARLOHDEE

There's a block to the left and a block to the right,
And a Bobo King in between,
Because FIBUA ops. is on tonight,
With Cheng Hu all over the scene.

That blerdy Sin Chiau's on my right,
Who always tuang and skive,
And I so shag, I tink I might,
Not come out of this alive.

Flat on der grass I feel so frus,
At brief I catch no ball.
I so blur, but I know I mus'
Wake up when the officer call.

I blank, I khoon, I got no hew,
My spirit has off the light,
Even I kena upside-down screw,
I wanna chicken and havoc tonight.

Lef' side one helicopter ed.,
He whisper someting to me,
And sardenly I no more dead,
He say, "Tink of your Arlohdee!"

I charge when der O.C. shout,
Soleed, man, I attack,
With tunder flashes I flush dem out,
At debrief dey pat my back.

Now all lecluits who got callup,
Kena liam keng from me,
"When you gabra and chuak and feeling feddup,
Tink of your Arlohdee!"

arm A rare one: The Singapore Arm Forces. Unarmed combat?

arrah As in *arrar-ee-see-arrah-you-eye-tee*: recruit; one of the lowest forms of animal life, we are told. One is a recruit when one joins the army and has not yet graduated to a private. Rank is of course a big thing in the army. If you have to send a message to a captain, however personal and confidential the matter may be, never mark it 'Private'.

The Chinese have no English *r* in their language, but have sounds that come close to it. There are no fundamental mental or physical blocks for a person whose mother-tongue is any dialect of Chinese to master the *r*, as there are for the Japanese to tackle the English *f* properly. The old jokes of *laundly* and *flied lice* give one a wrong impression. The Scots *r* of course is quite a different matter. But we must make it clear that Robbie Burns in Singapore is not Lobbie Burns, nor do our little ones say hickerly dickely dock.

We dreamt up a romantic possibility of a Singapore girl in England meeting a travelled Londoner who picks up her *r*, and changed the words of the song *Did your mother come from Ireland?*

DID YOUR MOTHER COME FROM ASIA?

Did your mother come from Asia?
'cos there's something in your talking,
Can you tell me where you got that Singlish arrh?
And before you left Toa Payoh,
Did your mother ever know,
That you finish every sentence with a lah?

> Tarling you're neet-peeking,
> And tarling I am steeking,
> To the sounds deep in my core.
> And you yourself you cannot drop,
> Your funny cockney glottalstop,
> So don't knock Singapore.
>
> Yes my mother's from Toa Payoh,
> And my frien' I'll have you know,
> You must love me with my Singlish,
> Dear Kwei Loh.

arrears When there's too much month left over at the end of the money Singaporeans go into odd *areas*.

Very common. *Er-rears* is the right sound, where *rears* is as in backs, or bottoms.

Arter The great king who sat at the head of the famous round table with his knights. The other English monarch, the one who burnt the cakes, doesn't come off any better in Singlish; he's Alfret.

But the English monarchs would probably get some consolation if they heard the Japanese version of General MacArthur which sounds like Dograss Makarser.

as The misuse of *as*, either by itself or with other words, is very common. Some examples:
He may be labelled as a snob.
As compare to ...
considered as a good piece ...
I speak Baba Malay. Is that considered as a dialect?

aspirate In the language of linguistics specialists the *h* is known as an aspirate since it must be pronounced with breathing. The Cockney accent drops the *h* and *Hampshire*, *Hartford* and *Herefordshire* becomes *'ampshire*, *'artford* and *'erefordshire*. There is a story of a member of parliament telling his friends after a hard day in the house, "I've got a 'ell of a 'eadache." F.E. Smith, who became Lord Chancellor, replied instantaneously, "What you need, Jim, is a couple of aspirates."

assure Quite frequent: *You can rest assure that ...* instead of the standard *You can rest assured that ...*

asterick Probably influenced by the comics. Heard now and then. More probably because those who say *asterisk* wrongly do not know how to spell it. It makes one wonder if the real problem is spelling.

at *Which hotel is he staying at?* There is nothing wrong with this sentence. We raise this and will be raising similar examples where there may be some doubt on whether the English is correct. The *BBC Guide* (ref. 3) makes a distinction of formality between the above sentence and *At which hotel is he staying?* and refers to the latter as more formal. Fowler in *A Dictionary of Modern English Usage* puts his advice on placing the preposition rather nicely:

"It was a cherished superstition that prepositions must be kept true to their name and placed before the word they govern in spite of the incurable English instinct for putting them late. If the final preposition that has naturally presented itself sounds comfortable, keep it."
Comfortable to the Singlish ear?

attach Fairly common: *I attach to First SIR.*
(SIR = Singapore Infantry Regiment)

back *I'll call you back* is Singlish for *I'll return your call* or *I'll call you later*.

This calling back is so ingrained in Singaporeans that the *Straits Times* of 13 May 1992 slipped *back* into a sentence: "Michael Jackson had called him back after watching his video which contained his illusions", referring to the first contact between Michael Jackson and Franz Harary.

bahse Bus in Singlish. One of the series mismouthing the *u* vowel. The letter *u* is pronounced in a great many ways; as in busy, bury, thud, beautiful, burr, bull and buy. Can Singlish not be excused if it does not handle *u* very well? Others in the series are baht, gass (guess what?), bahter, bahterflies, blahff, sahker, rahder (rudder or rather), mahd, cahddle, bahjet.

bahskate Basket with a Singlish *kate* in place of the English *kit*. After all, Catherine could be Kate or Kitty, couldn't she? The other untamed *kates* are blankate, gaskate, pockate.

This is also a cleaned-up version of *bastard*, used at times in the Australian sense of endearment or familiarity. Falling into disuse as Singaporeans are unabashed about calling 'a spate a spate' these days.

bahtaks Not that tribe of Christians who live around Lake Toba in Sumatra, who play chess and sing beautifully, but *buttocks*.

Bandung A city in Indonesia. In Singapore, the cry of *Bandung* at a food centre means you want *ice-Bandung*, a watery milk with rose syrup and a lump or two of ice. It is a lovely bright pink and wonderful in the heat of a Singapore afternoon. There are only a few influences of Indonesia, the giant at our doorstep, visible in Singapore – ice-Bandung is one of them. As far as Singlish is concerned, we have not been able to find anything of significance from Javanese or Bahasa Indonesia. We think this itself is significant.

barber-que Not an old Chinese word meaning barbers who specialise in queues, but the great outdoor burnt-meat thing. Again, Singlish shies away from putting the accent on the first syllable.

ARMY BARBER QUEUE

bare-loon Not a naked madman but a thin rubber bag filled with air mispronounced without fail at children's 'birt-day' parties.

base *Base on* or even *baze on* – very common. *Bazic* is part of the wretched family. *The project was base on every Singaporean eating five meals a day.*

A redundancy that occurs all over the world and appears in Singlish at times is *basic fundamentals*.

bears Years ago, when 'black-and-white' amahs were still around to fuss over and surreptitiously organise their expatriate bachelor bosses, a new arrival was alarmed when his amah reported "There were no bears in the fridge." Hiding his surprise he muttered "uh-uh", hoping she would go away so he could check out the fridge himself. But she insisted on pursuing the subject. "Tomollow Saturday and no bears in the fridge. Velly bad, sir. People will say this house no good. Must have bears for Saturday, Sunday. You gimme mahney, I go shop and buy two dozen bears." Beer is given its due respect in Singapore and not distorted these days. (*Black-and-white* for Singapore expatriates is no longer a domestic but the old government timbered houses.)

beeginning Apart from the occasional mispronunciation of the word, one often sees a failure to distinguish between start and beginning; the starting off, which is completed when it is executed and the beginning which is the first event of a series. The phrase from *The Sound of Music* illustrates the difference: "Let's start at the very beginning ..." Are we nitpicking?

Beethoven Pronounced in Singlish as it is spelt, with *bee* as the accented head of *Beethoven*. He would not like that. He was very conscious of his head, knowing that the source of his inspiration lay there. He believed that his brain was stimulated if he poured ice-cold water over his head while he was working (ref. 9).

beezy *Beezy, beezy bees ... beezy celling their honey*, Mr Oh (ref. 12) would say.

Benchen Our diminishing smoker friends tell us that in some places one should ask for Benchen if one needs Benson and Hedges. The bazaar language adapts to stupid sounding brand names. When Peter Stuyvesen arrived here, it was a horrifying new sound. The ingenuity of the bazaar language made it a friendly Peter. You order a pack of Peter, if that's what you want in Singapore. When nobody's looking, of course. It's quite sinful to smoke here.

better *Better you speak to him yourself.* Of the same genre as *after*, *also* – collapsing phrases into one word.

bit "Why you looking so sad, Mary?"
"Because I bit the dog just now."
"Bit the dog!"
"Yes lah; it was so naughty."
"But why bite it?"
"Bit lah; with a steek. I bit it with a steek lah."

The short English *i* so often becomes an *ee* in Singlish. There are many examples: "Doan lah! I teeklish dere." Shark's feen, nail cleepers, feefty meelion, pork leever, condense meek, neeple, seely boy, bull-sheet, rat-sheet.

> Singlish has three types of errors: pronunciation, grammar and vocabulary. Vocabulary is sometimes used quite incorrectly. We mean that Singlish has taken a word and given it another meaning and everyone believes that the usage in Singapore is correct. *Acronym* is an example.

blerd Bloody Singlish mispronunciation! Toh Paik Choo (ref. 20) gives two fine variations of the base word *blerd*. When used in anger with *hell*, it becomes, she says, *blaardy hail*, and that Singlish abbreviation for high blood pressure, she says, is *high blerd*, as in *He has high blerd*. In Singapore, the pressure is obvious so there is no need to say it. Nobody here has *high blerd* as in *blue blerd*. We are a republic.

blur Dunce, slow-witted. NS slang.

boastercock Braggart (getting obsolete). Braggarts on the other hand appear to be multiplying. It does conjure up a wonderful image of a cock crowing over its fellow cocks.

boss This word is never used to address the boss. It occurs as a friendly appellation in Singapore, somewhat like the Australian *mate* or the American *mister!* when calling out politely to someone one doesn't know. *Boss* was coined in the early colonial days of America. Many immigrants did not like the English term *master*, so they decided to use the Dutch *baas*, which means uncle.

bottom This story went around in the fifties at the time when the first elections to positions of limited power were stirring excitement in Singaporeans. Successful candidates, still blissfully unaware of the burdens of their office, went wild with exuberance and joy; one of them lost control of his sentence structure in his victory speech at the counting station. He ended it with "I thank you from the bottom of my heart and from my wife's bottom ... er ... of her heart."

bozo Clown. NS slang.

braid Eaten with butter and jam, honey or kaya; sometimes toasted. Should be pronounced *bred*, as in the raven to raven conversation: "Have you bred any good rooks lately?" Braid has its Singlish phonetic fellows, daid, said.

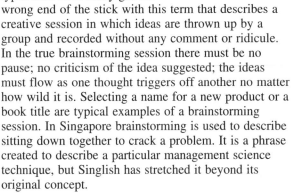

brainstorming Management types here have really got the wrong end of the stick with this term that describes a creative session in which ideas are thrown up by a group and recorded without any comment or ridicule. In the true brainstorming session there must be no pause; no criticism of the idea suggested; the ideas must flow as one thought triggers off another no matter how wild it is. Selecting a name for a new product or a book title are typical examples of a brainstorming session. In Singapore brainstorming is used to describe sitting down together to crack a problem. It is a phrase created to describe a particular management science technique, but Singlish has stretched it beyond its original concept.

brake The Singaporean, getting the maximum out of his vocabulary, uses the noun as a verb; usually a command. *Brake!* means *Stop!*

brarder *I got two brarder, one seester.*

brazier This item of women's clothing before Greer sparked off the great bra burnings used to be pronounced as if it were a container of glowing coals, but today's universal brief *bra* has squashed this little Singlish tidbit.

breakthrough Written Singlish often follows a common universal practice of putting redundant adjectives in front of *breakthrough*. Fowler points out that this word has military origins and a break through the enemy lines implied a collapse of the enemy front. He frowns on expressions like *major breakthrough*. To Fowler, a breakthrough is a breakthrough. Nothing could better a breakthrough.

bring-come A direct translation from the Chinese *na-lai*. There are a great many misuses of the verb *to bring* in Singlish, mostly arising from translating the Chinese *bring* which has very free rules of application. *I brought my girlfriend to the zoo* of course could be correct if one lives in the zoo. Similar errors occur in Philippinglish because the Tagalog verb *dala* is used for *bring* and *take*. Thus *bring there* and *take here* arise (ref. 11).

broat A *broat* education ... in Singlish? Heard daily on the air in 'Singapore Broatcasting Copperation' before it went defunct.

Is Singlish what Kipling once referred to as trade-English? See *caption*.

buaya Crocodile in Malay. It has two meanings in Singapore conversation today. One, among the young, is a skirt chaser. The other, on the golf course, is one who does not reveal his true handicap and takes bets on the game he and his *kaki* (group, friends) are about to play. Both meanings have the implication of chewing up or swallowing the opposition.

builup This is not a request to total up the bill. There is a standard Singapore cry for this: "Taber No. 6 beell!" which must be delivered with full lung power to rise above the clatter of plates, conversation and piped music. It's just that the *d* is swallowed in Singlish. Singlish just loves swallowing its *d*'s!

bum Just as you settle back in your seat after the aeroplane door is shut, and you feel the plane starting to move, you may get that familiar mentholated medicinal smell; and you know it's going to follow you for the next fifteen hours all the way to Europe. Then the Singapore lady sitting next to you offers you her *Tiger-bum*. If you're sensitive to mispronunciations and medicinal smells, when the one-two combination hits you, buzz immediately for a double whisky. If durians are banned on aeroplanes, why not Tiger-bum? Apart from the mispronunciation of *balm*, one also runs into *bum* in a sense that is not English slang but Singlish: *Alamak! I got bum off ... out of the team.*

buy-back, buy-back-home, buy-home The opposite of the American takeaway, and why not? It's the consumer's point of view, not the restaurateur's.

We believe it was used before *takeaway* was coined to distinguish the cooked food purchase from an order for food to be eaten on the spot. There is an occasional *buy-away* error. Crewe (ref. 5) gives an example: "Money cannot be used to buy away sickness and disease."

There is really no English equivalent to *buy-back*. The closest translation is probably the clumsy *buy it and take it home*. That's why the Americans (Chinese Americans?) coined *take away*. A parallel difference between the seller's and buyer's point of view came up one evening when a well known doctor was introduced to a friend. He said he was at Mount E (Mount Elizabeth Hospital) and added, "The rich man's hospital." Someone cut in at once, "The rich doctor's hospital."

bye-yer Buyer.

C

cahlie-pop An old, old one. A thorough distortion of *curry-puff*; not Carly Simon, the pop-star of bygone days.

Cambridge Pronounced as though to point out that the University is a major cam in the British education machine. One of those funny English town names and surname pronunciations. The first syllable is pronounced as the past tense of come, *came*. (The river Cam is pronounced cam, as the piece of machinery. The English have tried for centuries to confuse foreigners with people and place names.)

can lah! There is no grammar or pronunciation error in this phrase but the newcomer to the region should be aware of its relaxed and imprecise use. If it is used in answer to the question "Can you fix my car radio?" it could mean that the responder can actually do it, but it could also mean that the technician does not want to displease you and though he's not quite sure, he's going to have a go at it. And probably have some fun.

cannibarl *One human body will feed twenty cannibarls.* Rare to medium-rare – in occurrence. Not discussed much these days. Did you know that an average man would serve about 60 cannibals, though not heartily? (Ref. 2)

The word *cannibal* reminds us of a discussion after a hearty meal of beef noodles. One of our friends criticised our repeatedly talking of our new Singlish finds. "You ought to be grateful that we just do variations on a sound English base," he said. "Look at Papua New Guinea. Look at what they have done to English. Cooked up a completely new language which is quite unintelligible to anyone who speaks English. You have to learn the darn thing, man."

He went on to give examples: *Miz-queen's number one piccaninny-boy* is Prince Charles. *Him-big-black-fellow-with-the-white-teeth-hit-him-in-the-teeth-he-cry* is a piano.

Is there a similarity between Singlish and Indian varieties of English? See *ellow*.

caption We actually read this bit in a letter about five years ago: ... *Further to our recent negotiation on the above captioned* ... This is one of the sad faces of Singlish. Written Singlish lags behind the spoken word by many years. There are still people around who believe that business letters and official reports should be laced with olde-world business jargon. As far back as 1973 *Reader's Digest* contained an article 'Write the way you talk' and pushed the point home with "Some human being will read your letter." We thought Rudyard Kipling had dealt the death blow to business jargon years ago in *The Village that Voted the Earth was Flat* with "He spoke and wrote trade-English – a toothsome amalgam of Americanisms and epigrams." (Ref. 4.)

Has Asian humility made it necessary to modify English? See *don't mind.*

carpate, carpet Incidentally, *carpet* is one of the words in English that has no rhyming partner. Others are purple, silver, spirit, chimney, liquid, and window. Watch it if you're composing a poem to your ladylove. Especially if she was in a purple dress with silver earrings standing on a Persian carpet by the window, looking out at the chimneys, her eyes, liquid and glinting with her carefree, wild spirit. Poets beware. Be aware.

carrier *She put her carrier before her love life.* Singaporeans above sixty would remember a Singlish word for a stack of three or more containers; the tiffin carrier. *Tiffin* was lunch. The word's dead. The tiffin carrier's been killed by plahsteek bags. (But she didn't put her tiffin carrier before her love life although she was Singaporean.)

carry on Another of those past tense problems: "Sometimes we Singaporeans are so bad. The udderday at the hawker centre we sardenly heard screams and cries of 'rape! rape!' but the man sitting next to me, he deeden even look up. He jes sat dere and carry on his meal."

"Den what happen?"

"Narting lah!"

"What did you do?"

"Why should I? Not my business what."

Note what many Singaporeans continue to call the new food centres, where the MOE (Ministry of the Environment, not Education) has centralised the cooked food vendors who used to wander around the streets hawking, Hawkers Centres.

Another *carry* misuse: *I was interested in history so I carry out the course at the university.*

catch hold *See if you can catch hold of Ah Beng before he leaves.* This does not mean to grab him physically. Singlish redundancy.

category The more common mispronunciation puts the accent on the *gory* bit, but we have heard a version that sounds like *catagory* with the stress to the *tag*. A rare find.

caterlic Mishandled for both the Roman type and the universal.

CATS Committee for the Attraction of Talent to Singapore. There is no complimentary Retention of All Talent in Singapore project.

certifikate It's a shame that something so highly rated in Singapore should be badly pronounced! Singlish puts no accent on it. The accent should be on the second syllable.

champurisation A crossbreed of Malay and English, meaning a crazy mixture or a real odd concoction. Falling into disuse.

cheat-chat General; not only for business chats with con-men.

cheeky There is a special usage of *cheeky* in Singlish. Crewe (ref. 5) gives an example: *That man is very* *cheeky, you know; he grinned at me and asked me for a date.* Maybe out of date.

cheellee Usually pronounced the Malay way. But don't the English say it wrong?

> **If a Singlish-man tells you he lives in Boh-liao Road, where does he live? See *Dunearn*.**

chiak chuah NS slang. Play truant. From the Hokkien *to eat snakes*.

chiak loh! Hokkien expression brought into Singlish to make up for the absence of an English equivalent of *bon-appétit*. Somehow the English never found it necessary to create a phrase to wish their fellow diners enjoyment of the food they were about to eat, although they have numerous genteel and hearty expressions of good luck and health that precede drinking of their excellent beers and ciders. There is a Singlish expression which has not quite the same general application as *bon-appétit*. It is *join me*, used when one is eating and meets a friend, or if one starts eating while another is around but not eating.

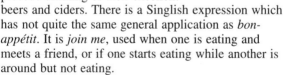

chin-chye Generally used with the hang-loose suffix *lah*. It means "Don't worry about the little details … lah." A sort of slapdash *as-long-as-it-works* phrase. Foreigners who have read books on our political history should note that the phrase does not come from the name of our past Deputy Prime Minister, Dr Toh Chin Chye. He was a man who devoted much effort to scrutinising details. He would hold no truck with *chin-chye, lah*.

Chinese Sometimes pronounced with *s*, as it is spelt, instead of the correct *Chineze*.

Chinese backside You can be fooled by this one. Not because the derrière of the Chinese is different. This refers to the haircut the army gives to recruits. NS slang.

chirren A lazy 'children'.

Chivas Legal The original; not an illegal adulterated bottle.

choot Although not very common, this is a delightful Singlish mispronunciation; one says it with the first syllable rhyming with *chew*, and the second with *hoot*. The two syllables are almost merged into one. It has to be shot out, in a staccatissimo burst. It conveys the image of garbage rushing down a sixteen-storey HDB rubbish chute – much better than the smooth slow RP pronunciation does. Did you know that the correct pronunciation is *shoot*?

chop The rubber stamp of a company name or a director's designation, in which so much faith is placed. It is treated with the same importance which is placed on the carved seals of old China and Japan, although one can get a rubber stamp made for a few dollars without any questions on whether one has the authority to order a stamp with that company name.

Chop is also used as a verb, as in *That fellow, the immigration lady, she wink at me while she chopped my passport.* (*Fellow* has bisexual applications in Singlish.)

chope To *chope* is to reserve or book a seat, a place, or a thing. Obsolete Singlish. Chope cannot be applied to a woman in the sense of *spoken for*.

Chopin The poor man is hewed, hacked and chopped into pieces in Singapore, along with his predecessor, Bach. Mr Oh (ref. 12) illustrates one of the many Singlish pronunciations: "Out Chopin. Will be Bach at two."

chowkah Hokkien for miser, Cantonese for dirty rascal, *chowkah* describes anything that is of inferior quality. Sneaked into Singlish.

church Tongue (ref. 21) points out the failure to distinguish the use of words like church which have special meanings. One can say *He has gone to church* but not *He has gone to City Hall* in the same sense. (In fact one should not say *He has gone to church to pray* unless there is a suspicion that he has gone there to look at the girls.) Tongue gives two examples of correct usage:
They have gone to church for the Thanksgiving Service.
He's gone to the church to leave a message for the vicar.

close the door A subtle difference not often realised in Singapore between *shutting* and *closing*. One also often hears "Close the tap." One of our linguistic friends pointed out to us that the sign *Close On Sunday* was fairly common. But remote and standoffish on other days?

clotes Do not confuse with *garrment*: "It was terrible! He was having a big fight with his wife; shouting an' all. Then the maid started taking off her clotes." See Toh Paik Choo (ref. 19). The correct pronunciation is *kloz*. With regard to the *form*, the question of when it is proper for domestics to remove their clothing in the heat of an argument is a socio-moral issue that we are unable to comment on.

cluster Rare, but has been heard *circa* 1981: "Eeh! Please don't cluster up the corridor."

cock-up It is with a certain reticence we comment on this NS expression listed in the *Straits Times* on National Day, 1991. (Incidentally the word *straits* in the name of the newspaper comes from the Straits Settlements – of Singapore, Malacca and Penang – and has no connotations of self-censorship.) The translation of the expression was *foul-up*. Society over the healing passage of time accepts expressions like cock-up, screwed-up and bloody, forgetting the origins; for example, *bloody* is derived from *By our Lady*, meaning *Mother of Christ*.

cocktail *I have a cocktail tonight.* One of the economy-of-breath characteristics of Singlish, leaving out the *party*. Or maybe he's only going to have one drink?

coddinate, cor-ordinate The Singlish telescoping of sounds. *C'llect* is a close relation.

Cola bears This is not a new un-classical Coke. It is the Australian Koala (without the *bear*) transformed in Singlish to a sound that rolls off the tongue without dwelling on the *ah* of it all. Ah! Those amazing Australian mammals who don't drink!

cole As in "Come here tarling (the Chinese phonetic version), hole me ... I so cole ..." Air conditioning in Singapore is so often too cold.

come on *Come on, man!* is used where the English would use *Come off it.*

complexion Heard on 'Dateline': "I'm a fair complexion." Most Singaporeans do not realise that the usage of *fair* and *dark* in the UK is quite different from that in Singapore. The English would refer to a person with black hair and a porcelain-white skin as *dark*, and a blonde sunburnt to a well done toast-brown would be called *fair*. It's the hair colour that counts in the UK when they say a person is fair or dark.

computer *I'm studying computer. Personal computer is our business.* Very, very often used when *computers* should be used.

consider *Let me think about it. I have to consider about the distance from Bedok to Jurong.* (Distance relativity to the Singaporean is something that expatriates have to adjust to.) While Singlish ignores the *it* that must come after *appreciate*, it often inserts *about it* after *consider*.

con-tro-ver-sy Spoken with just a touch of stress on *ver*. There is some controversy on this word in the UK. It is one of those words that is being pronounced differently by some these days. When doubts arise, the *BBC Guide* (ref. 3), which was written to guide BBC staff in 1981, is most useful. It recommends the stress on the first syllable, following the style of *matrimony* rather than *monopoly*, 'the traditional stressing'.

convicted A gem we heard at an interview of a graduate applicant for a teaching job.
"Are you quite sure you want to be a teacher?"
"Yes. After doing relief teaching I was quite convicted that I want to be a teacher."

coobooks, cook books Cooking books ? Or cooked books?

cooling The complement of *heaty*. See **heaty**.

copulator True story of a Singapore child's slip:
"My mother brought a copulator home last night."
"A WHAT!? What did your father say?"
"He says it makes lovely coffee."

cornered beef An old one going out of fashion. It came from the days when a lot of corned beef in those trapezoidal cans was eaten. They did have rounded corners.

corporal A prize piece in our collection. A young graduate relief teacher was relating her experiences in the classroom. "They are terrible sometimes. One day I got so mad I nearly administered capital punishment." She jolly well knew no teacher is allowed to 'administer' *corporal* punishment. We have also heard references to corporate punishment in schools.

coss "Have you included the overhead coss?" "Ovcoss I have."

cosset An early Edwardian Singlish mispronunciation. Such things have gone now that aerobics and jogging keep Singapore feminine tummies under control. We are glad the word is no longer in use. There is such a vast difference between a lover cosseting the delicate apple of his eye and the draper or middle-aged husband strenuously corsetting a plumpish woman.

cot As in *squash cots* of the 'spotty' set. Or *cots* in which judges sit.

Judges sit in cots.

course The Singlish abbreviation *He's on course* means he's attending a course. And the plural is zedded to *courzes*.

coy Talking to a principal of a school, we heard him refer to his *coy mistress* with some surprise. How charming and honest, we thought to ourselves. But not for long. It soon became evident that she was in fact his school *choir* mistress; who is not what Andrew Marvell wrote about.

crack Singaporeans sometimes say *crack his brains* instead of the English expression *crack his head* (ref. 21).

craps Don't be put off by an invitation to eat *craps* or *chilli-craps*. It's just some version of mixed crabs.

criet *She was so shock! Criet and all.* Self-explanatory.

cup-board Enunciated as two distinct syllables: a prime example of not knowing that a letter in the English spelling is mute. Does this sort of error arise from first meeting the word on paper rather than from an oral introduction? We think it does. There are so many examples of the mute consonants being enunciated only because no one has told them that they are mute.

We throw out a challenge to the reader to make up a short story or a poem using all the common English words that have a mute consonant. We tried and failed. We got such odd sentences: *She rushed to the cupboard where she kept her salmon and almonds when she saw the plumber and the almoner fall into the Thames.*

dack, deck. Present-day Singlish just cannot handle the *e*. Almost all *e* sounds are pronounced *a*. Related to *dack* are batter (better), devalopment, 'A' lavals, spacialist, compatitors, vatinary, tacknikal, ralavent, stap.

dam Merely referring to a moist condition, without annoyance. Singlish so often ignores the terminal consonant.

dahsty, dusty Note that *dust* is one of those English words that has opposite meanings. *To dust the crops* is really the opposite of *to dust the piano*. *Cleave* is similar.

dat A member of the *dat*, *dese*, *dose*, *dere* series. The *th* sound which was no problem to the last generation has been lost. De udders are *tree tousand*, *tink* about all sorts of *tings*, I had a *teak* steak, his *ties* are so strong. He was torn between Rosie and *Pillipa*, sitting between dem like a rose between two *torns*.

Dayvit The little fellow who defeated Goliat. This is one of a Singlish family of errors. The terminal *d* takes too much effort. The sound that comes out is a cross between *d* and *t*; but more *t* to our ears.

Hurt in the Singapore Cricket Club: *There's no rest for the wicket ... a weeg is worn on the het, you stupit fellow ... towarts ... dat Howart so prout lah! ... I hat stoot waiting for tirty minutes ... you can get advise on consumer's tastes all over the world at the World Trait Centre ... han-bak ...*

debb-ters No one seems to have told accountants and bookkeepers in Singapore that there is a mute consonant in *debtors*. It should be pronounced *dettors*. True Singlish speakers will not appreciate Mr Oh's (ref. 12) pun: "To love and to cherish till debt do us part."

deceased This is not pronounced incorrectly, nor is it mishandled grammatically in Singlish, but we suspect it has been saturated with Chinese immortality connotations. We see in the papers the notices of death that read like this:

"Tan XY passed away peacefully in his sleep on zz.zz.19zz ... mourned by his sons Albert, Gregory, Bernard ... his daughters Eileen, May Lin, Mary (deceased)."

Singlish is sometimes quite creative. See *ever*.

delivered A Singlish version has the accent on *del* very strongly; it sounds like *dell* (where the farmer lives) or the first syllable of Delhi. This is almost without exception an Indian tongue distortion which makes us wonder if there are not three or more subvarieties of Singlish; Sino-Singlish, Malay-Singlish, Indo-Singlish and others.

dep *We are making an in-dep study of the problem.* Reports seem to refer to any study as an *in-dep* one.

desert Be aware that this may not always be a sandy wasteland. It could be the sweet finale of dinner. But of course, the last course, dessert, is pronounced *de-zert*.

detach Very common: *a detach house*. It is a distant relative of the *air-condition*. Detached houses with air-conditioners must be a nightmare to those English expatriate teachers we have brought here to help us straighten out the kinks in the language of Byron, Scott, Shelley and Keats while they are house-hunting.

development A particular fault of Indo-English is to put the accent on the first syllable and often, but not always, pronounce it *dav*. Non-Indian Singaporeans prefer *devalopment*.

Dezember A tracer word. If you hear Dezember in any place in any part of the world, turn round and meet a Singaporean.

die for you You've had it, mate. This Singlish pessimistic prognosis is a direct translation of a much used Chinese phrase which seems to be especially forceful in the Hokkien *Lu see loh!* It has deep connotations. It reflects the abhorrence of death and anything connected with it. To predict that your mate is going to die for whatever indiscretion she or he has committed is the most frightening scenario one can throw out. Although this is not quite in concord with the Buddhist attitude to death, it is the prevalent subconscious attitude in Singapore where much lip service is paid to Buddhism.

dieded Singlish accentuation of the finality of death.

dilemma Singaporeans are usually in a *dilemma* on the pronunciation of this word. The *BBC Guide* (ref. 3) recommends the stress on the first syllable with a short *i*, NOT as in *die*.

dirty *Dirty* is spat out in a very special way by mothers who see their children pick something up from the floor. It is difficult to describe the sound in words; somewhere between *dirdy*, *ditty* and *duddy* – all said very fast and in a chiding tone.

Singaporeans handle dirt quite adequately. There may be a psycho-socio-linguistic reason. But while we are on the unpleasant subject of dirt, we will take this opportunity, as commercials on TV do, to encourage the reader who has reached *D* and is beginning to wilt by quoting to her or him the Earl of Chesterfield: "Words are the dress of thoughts, which should no more be presented in rags, tatters and dirt, than your person should."

discuss Singlish constantly forgets that the verb *discuss* must have an objective. One cannot just discuss. You have to discuss something, even if you leave it as vague as ever with discuss *it*.

disinterested There is a common failure to distinguish between *un*interested and *dis*interested. This is not only a Singapore fault. We mention it because the *BBC Guide* states that the incorrect use of these words attracted more unfavourable comment than any other word concerning usage, with the possible exception of *hopefully*.

dock Overheard, a schoolboy conversation:
"I saw a dock in the canal yesterday."

"A dock! A floating dock!"
"No lah! A dead dock lah!"

doe Sometimes heard; meaning door. This sound could change that *Sound of Music* song. We tried to see how it could be Singlish-ed:

> Do' a door, a Singlish door,
> Ray, of the sun of Singapore,
> Mee, rebus or Hokkien mee,
> Far, from Jurong to Johor.
> Ah Soh, sister of Ah Koh,
> La, after every 'no',
> Tea, instead of kopi-oh,
> which brings us back to Do'.

don't mind To oblige. Used in the old days as a respectful opener for touching someone for a fiver or a favour by those who had not got past primary school. Not being used any more as this sort of obsequious approach is being replaced by the direct American/Australian style. Sometimes the open approach is preceded with the Singlish, "Frankly, is like this …"

don'tch A rather rare variant of *doan*. We are not sure if it really means *don't touch*.

down There is a great tendency to add *up* or *down* after verbs of movement in and out of Singapore. It's not always dependent on the north or south juxtaposition of the country concerned with Singapore.

We think saying someone has *come down here* has an element of inferiority in it. At Oxford and Cambridge the expressions are to *go up* to the university and to *come down* for holidays or after graduation. One is *sent down* if one misbehaves.

There was a similar tendency to use *up* in such phrases as *I rang her up*, but this seems to be going out of fashion as dropping the *up* has come in. See **pick**.

downstair Not just one step down; in Singlish it means all the way down.

dring *It was a good party. There was plenty to eat and dring.* The shy end consonant, refusing to raise its rightful voice.

duck They were lying flat on their stomachs in the prickly grass under a thick bush, tense, watching the jungle path in front of them. Ming Kang felt an ant crawling up his trousers but he didn't flinch. He couldn't show Ah Fatt lying beside him that he was soft. He lay there ready, finger on the trigger. He was not going to let his platoon down, whether it was a mock ambush or the real thing. They would fight side by side. In six months he had learnt it all. He was no longer a recruit. He was a combat man; a man gripping his gun; yah, a MAN.

Suddenly Ah Fatt said, "Duck." Ming Kang dropped his head down at once. But nothing happened. He waited a few seconds. Then he stretched his neck and looked up. He couldn't see a thing in the pre-dawn darkness.

"Sheesh! Ah Fatt, what did you see?"
"Narting lah."
"Then why you say 'duck'?"
"Duck lah. So duck I can't see a ting lah."

Dun-nyern Singapore rightly prides itself as one of the few ex-colonial nations that did not scratch out the names of places and streets of men with imperfect histories. Yet one feels at times that the relevant authorities (one always puts *relevant* before *authorities* here, presumably because of the ever-present danger of the matter being dealt with by irrelevant authorities) should have changed the names of roads that Singaporeans find difficult to pronounce. The only one attempt that seems to have been made in this direction is *Bays Water Road*.

Dunearn falls into this group that presents pronunciation difficulties. We are sure that great men like him and Clemenceau would understand if we removed their names from our streets and avenues and would not feel too much pain. Bless them.

Other names that one must enquire about in the local accent are Daliah, Berwick, Warwick, Netheravon, Worcester; and particular concentration is required to recognise Pepys and Beaulieu, not confusing the last with Hokkien.

We had a bad experience when our car broke down on Dunearn Road and the AAS man told us there was no such road in his street directory. Our deliberate mispronunciation brought the "Ah!" of recognition.

economics Singlish pronounces it neither in the English e-ko-nom'iks way, nor in the American, e-karn-ner-miks way.

> **Economy of breath; that's what Singlish is all about. True? Read on.**

eechie A Singlish adjective which is dying out is *eechified*; meaning a girl who has men dominant on her mind. The restless meaning most probably comes from the Malay *gatal* which has connotations beyond 'scratchy'.

eemply Imply. *Imply* and *infer* are often confused not only in Singapore but even in the UK. A.P. Herbert in *What a Word!* explains the distinction: "If you see a man staggering along the road you may infer that he is drunk, without saying a word; but if you say, 'Had one too many?' you do not infer but imply that he is drunk."

effluent Quite often mixed up with affluent. Crewe cites the example, *effluent society – the stinking rich*.

ellow An Indian version of *yellow*. While they tend to drop the *y* in yellow, they make up for it by adding one to India: Yindia. R.K. Tongue (ref. 21) raises an interesting question about how similar English errors he found in India were to those of Malaysia and Singapore. Did they come from India or did they arise independently in the two regions? We don't know. We do know that the 'Ceylon Burghers', the mixed bloods who came from Ceylon, brought with them English, Dutch, Singhalese and Tamil words which identified them, and some of these words were absorbed into the local English of the prewar Colonial days. Many of them were teachers.

emphasise *We need to emphasise on ...* Singlish inserts a redundant *on*.

enjoy From a teacher genuinely dedicated to her job: "Only eef I give the guys books with some adventure and excitement will they enjoy." The verb *enjoy* seems to have taken on new variations. An English press-woman sent us a note giving us details of the restaurants around where we would be staying in London and ended it with 'Enjoy!' With no object. Grammatically, that is.

envelope Two pronunciations occur in Singlish. It may interest you to know that the BBC prefers the one in which the first syllable rhymes with *ten* to the version in which it rhymes with *on*.

EO If you deal with the government you should note that there may be civil servants at the end of the phone line who would not recognise the words *executive officer*. It is safer to use their *EO* abbreviation. Or use *exey-cute-ive*.

establish Quite common: *I could not establish a rapport with her.* That's why they have the SDU (Social Development Unit), to bring the males and 'ladies' together. (See **lady**.)

even In Singlish, *even* appears at the end of a sentence to add emphasis. From *The Pick of Paik Choo*: "Know what I like to know? The names of the tailors the male participants go to. You saw their outfits? Gee whiz, man, dressy, fancier than the girls' clothes even."

ever *I ever read Jane Austen.* The complement of *I've never read Jane Austen.* Quite ingenious, actually. Very common. So is the reading of Jane Austen because of the regular inclusion of a Jane Austen in school texts. And because they do enjoy her novels. We wonder if there is any significance in this. Does the old Chinese and Malay impregnable pride of our Singapore girls keep meeting the immovable prejudice of our boys? Singlish also misuses *ever* in the context *ever since* at times. The implication of the events continuing to happen when *ever since* is used is often not appreciated. If this is not appreciated all over the world, should we nail Singlish with this one?

expatriate Expatriates are usually given the *stay* and *pay* sound treatment. The *pat* treatment is seldom applied. We believe that either the *pat* or the *pay* may be used. (Singaporeans these days use the brief *expat*.)

expect We came across this cryptic answer to a written questionnaire for job applicants. In reply to the question, "Why do you want this job?" the applicant wrote, "… could earn as much as you can expect."

fack A four-letter word sometimes treated without the correct finish by Singaporeans, as in *the facks of life*. Today the fax of life have a new urgency.

fallowship It makes the heart of every taxpayer bleed to hear that academic and medical people are going overseas on government funds for a two-year *fallowship*. Imagine them lying fallow, taken out of the production system like fields, yielding nothing for two years!

fantas An abbreviation of fantastic; obsolete?

Feb-you-ary The BBC prefers *Febroori* (ref. 3).

Fee-oh-nix Rising out of the ashes of English – the phoenix.

fetch Fetch is one of the most misused words in Singlish. A typical error is "Get a taxi to fetch you to the airport."

fierce Meaning *unusual*, *terrific*, *great* in NS slang.

filim Film. The double consonant is very difficult for any human being, including Singaporeans.

finish already "Have you done your homework?" "Finish already lah!"

This is a direct translation from the Chinese which has a suffix, a monosyllabic character *le*, that puts the past tense into a verb. It does, however, give a stronger sense of completion to *finish* that can only be conveyed in English by tone of voice.

fiscal fitness Not one's ability to pay tax, but the condition aimed at by regular taxing of one's muscles.

fiss Not heard very often. It used to be a speciality of Hainanese waiters. But today one is sometimes offered a real low calorie dish: *fish and chip*.

We repeat the old one about the schoolboy who defended his spelling of *fish* to illustrate the problems of pronunciation and spelling in English. He spelt it *ghit*, and explained it was *gh* as in *tough* and *ti* as in *notion*.

fissead We love fissead. We write this salivating. It is something that is very good in Singapore. It has a thousand variations. Even in pronunciation. *Fissead carlie* is one.

fitter One of a whole series of mispronunciations of those deceitfully servile men bred in the colonial past who have struggled valiantly to provide the British first, and later a whole host of strange white men, with the cuisine of their homelands. They give service with an air close to the eighteenth century models imposed on them, and have subjected their sharp Hainanese minds, lips and tongues to the contortions of speaking English.

Fitter would be understood if one hears it after an excellent Hainanese chicken curry, and *banana fitter* is offered to round off the meal.

We cannot resist the temptation to relate a recent incident in a well known club when a visitor, overcome by the smiling service and efficiency of the greying waiter, overrating his position in the scheme of things Singaporean, asked him to recommend a wine to go with his *biftake*. The waiter, aware of his language limitations, rose to the occasion admirably. He recommended the house wine. There was no way he could manage the pronunciation of Latour, Pinot, Chardonnay. He might have handled the Australian Lee-Singham (Leasingham) but he probably didn't think the bouquet was right for the *biftake*. We think he deserves a medal.

fiyer *Where there's smok, there's fiyer.*

> The idea that English in Singapore is, if not a de facto national language, something much more than a 'dominant working language', has been advanced by a number of people. —Joseph Foley (ref. 6).

flerd Flood mispronounced. The PWD (Public Works Department) has reduced the frequency of this error by reducing flooding in Singapore.

flow-were The same Singlish is used for the objects of inspiration to painters and poets and to the raw material of inspiration to pastry chefs.

fluke shot A chance shot. May be dying out. *Fluke* is a noun. It can be a fluke; but not a fluke shot.

food No book on any aspect of Singapore would be complete without mentioning food. So we have to, although there are no linguistic problems with the word food. Singaporeans can cope with almost all forms and variations of food; in fact they also mix them with an admirable spirit of enquiry and exploration of the unknown. Much more than they mix words and sounds. The poem below conveys some of this rojak (a Malay salad) spirit.

DOOF, DOOF, BEAUTIFUL DOOF

I voel the doof of Singapore,
In dam demix manes.
Naw-not-eem and mee-enggore,
Char-wise-wops in side lanes.

Hillic chicken and hillic bracs,
Prata-tori and shif curry,
Pink-red pork gels on the racks,
Pig tails and Nohekki mee.

Kalsa, red and hillic hot,
Drastoe ducks with thick gravy,
Feeb or sprawn in caly pot,
Gumharbers, big and KFC

Such lovely sword,
And tasty shides,
Pu-mixed in my belly,
Delicious doof and zarcy sounds,
Will be the thead of me!

Solution: food; love; mad; mixed; names; wan-ton-mee; mee-goreng; char-siew-pows; chilli; crabs; roti-prata; fish; legs; Hokkien mee; laksa; roasted; beef; prawns; clay; hamburgers; words; dishes; mixed-up; crazy; death.

fool Heard quite often: *Doan play a fool with me lah!* The verb *to fool* is often subjected to past tense errors. *A lot of experts have been fool.*

forfeet Not a quadruped, but a playful penalty.

> Singlish has often taken in an Asian word that has no equally expressive equivalent in English. See *gerderbook.*

four-dee This is a Singapore and Malaysian addiction that causes traffic jams. It is gambling on the last four digits of the horse racing sweepstake. In accordance with the Singlish practice of economy of sounds *digit* becomes *D*. Traffic jams are caused by drivers slowing down to look at the number plates of vehicles involved in accidents. These are reckoned to be the lucky numbers to bet on. And the guiding principle is the bloodier the accident, the luckier the number.

free A misuse of *free* in the context of *free-time* which occurs fairly often is *I'm very free with my time these days.*

free gift Does this redundancy occur only in Singapore?

frien An abbreviation of *friend* or *befriend*, the verb: *I won't frien you!*

froks "My daughter wants to buy a frok. Where to buy?"
"Metro's is a good place for frocks."
"No lah! Don't be so blurr. A frok lah! A jumping frok."
"Ah! A playsuit!"

furnish There is a strong tendency to use *furnish*: *Furnish me with a little more informations*. And *to furnish* is subjected to the widespread mangling of past tenses and indirect speech. A common phrase is *furnish flat*, as in *He has moved to a furnish flat*.

With Singlish being what it is, how about poetry? See graduates.

G

gastric *I have gastric.* Quite painful to the grammatically sensitive.

gent Public toilets fascinate us. Not the activity nor the types one meets and exchanges pleasantries with while … but the mundane physical details. We were overjoyed when the humdrum *Straits Times* actually went out on a campaign to search out the bad and the beautiful. Yes, there are some which are quite, quite beautiful.

We had one funny experience at the Shangri-la toilet. (We, by the way, are male.) That wonderful little bit of high-tech had just been installed, a little red light that goes on as one stands and delivers. As you walk away there's a subdued musical rush of water; the darn thing flushes itself. Well, one day we were there letting our hair down, so to speak, after a goodly consumption of Singapore Tigers, when we noticed from the accents that we were standing, not quite cheek by jowl, but almost hip to hip to a long line of Americans. We heard an alcoholic voice ask, "What's with this red light?" We couldn't resist the temptation and replied to the line at large, "This is a new high-tech job. It checks you up while you're there, bared. If you're OK, you get a green light." We left with a smirk and a zippy, uppety feeling.

But we have digressed. We want to tell you about a singular public toilet in Toa Payoh. It is a sort of a personal one. About two metres wide, it can cope with the stoutest and finest of men. It was a surprise to us; there in Toa Payoh, the one-person service; the public toilet for you alone, labelled *Gent*.

gentiles In Singapore we censor any part of a film that shows the gentiles. Nothing pro-Semitic about this.

gentleman Often mispronounced; but being rightly discarded by the younger Singaporeans. Fowler (ref. 7) compares it to the outdated *Esquire*. "Our use of *gentleman*, like that of *Esquire*, is being affected by our progress towards a classless society, but in the opposite way; we are all esquires now, and we are none of us gentlemen any more."

gerderbook-gerderbak A really forceful onomatopoeic Malay phrase that just rolls off the tongue. It indicates sudden surprise. Seldom heard in Singlish today. Pity.

giddy Tongue (ref. 21) has something to say on *giddy*: "Heights make me giddy; if I feel giddy I see a doctor. Strong drink makes people dizzy in SEUK (Standard English of the United Kingdom). One hears ESM (English of Singapore and Malaysia) say 'Drinks make me feel giddy.'" The last bit about what Singaporeans say is generally correct; in the physical and not the frivolous sense.

gift of the gab We really chuckled over this one. It seemed such an apt error; probably a typing error and not a Singlish howler. A report on a dentist, an orthodontics specialist, contained the line, *She has the gift of the gap.*

> Perhaps we should have two Singlishes – one written and one spoken? See *manage.*

girl Babas and Eurasians very often address their children as *girl* or *boy*. It is strange to hear a child whom the parents have, with great deliberation and due consideration of their ancestors' names, the ruling film stars' names, saints' names and the special powers attributed to individual saints, named Theresa Marie Josephina Raquel de Souza, being yelled for with *Girl!* The cuter ones are called *girlie*. The Peranakans and Eurasians also use *sonny*. It's going out of fashion with the success of the Japanese electronic company's marketing programme.

give off Fairly frequently one hears the Singlish *give off* or *give out*, which we think comes from the Chinese suffix verb *choo*. Crewe's example (ref. 5) is: "If one does not respect one's employers one does not give off one's best." Equally popular is *give of one's best*.

gone case A hopeless case.

goondu Fool. Do not confuse with *lembu* which only applies to stupid learner drivers. *Lembu* is cow in Malay.

Gord A deity. Actually this peculiar pronunciation of *God* is only mouthed by those who have a standard of pronunciation well above the average in Singapore and are stretching to reach perfection. (True blue Singaporeans would use *axcellence* these days.)

Gord is a telltale sign. Over-sounding of some vowels and incorrect stress, not on the syllables within words, but on wrong words in sentences, are characteristics of this small intense group. Stressing the words within a sentence is a second-degree skill which comes after one has mastered the stresses within words, which those who are trying to speak perfect RP sometimes do not realise. Getting the accents on individual words right does not mean you have arrived.

got So often used incorrectly. Tongue (ref. 21) gives an example of this substandard English:
"Have you got a pen?"
"Got."
"Have you got a pencil?"
"Also got."
"Got or not?"

Other examples:
I got the long hair.
This place got Malay food or no'? I wan to eat that kuning fish. Dunno good or no' here. (Note the Malay for yellow, *kuning*, has crept in.)

graduates Pronounced so that the last syllable rhymes with *grates*. Such errors provoked a *frien* to postulate that Singaporeans will never appreciate nor produce outstanding *poh-yems* in English because of mispronunciations. But he was rebutted by an equally inebriated *frien* who pointed out that mispronunciations did not matter; as long as they were consistent. "After all," he said, "a 'frok' can rhyme with a 'dock'."

And Coleridge can still be appreciated in Singlish …

> I moved my leeps, the Pilot shrieked
> And fell down in a feet;
> The holy Hermeet raised his eyes,
> And prayed where he did seet.

Singlish often takes an English noun and uses it as a verb. See *horn, brake*.

gotten JC students have revived this archaic past participle meaning *got* and many parents have adopted the curiosity.

grandfarder's An old Singlish expression that is, we believe, unique. *Your grandfarder's* is a bring-them-back-to-reality device in reductio-ad-absurdio logic. If someone is cycling carefree and abandoned in the middle of the road, one would shout out, "Your grandfarder's road ah!" If she suggests that Tyersall Palace grounds would be a nice place to wander into and smooch, one would say, "Your grandfarder's place ah." The expression is dying with our grandfarders.

graps "I cannot graps the meaning." Heard many times. The Singlish diversion to avoid the terminal consonant *p*.

guynee Not heard as often in Singapore as *O & G*. Medical and technical terms also have their local favourites; and they change with time. The *BBC Guide* (ref. 3) describes how gynaecology started at about 1898 with a soft *g* till about 1930 when both the soft and hard *g*'s were used and from about 1930 the hard *g* took over completely. (Personally we think the soft *g* is more appropriate.) We can list a lot of mispronounced technical words but that would be getting into too much specialisation.

guys Girls sometimes address each other with "You guys …" Is this a universal new bisexual usage?

gynotikolobomassophile This is not yet a Singlish word. It comes from that book by Josefa Heifetz Byrne (Pocket Books), *Mrs Byrne's Dictionary of Unusual, Obscure and Preposterous Words*. It means one who likes to nibble at a woman's earlobe. In Greek, *gyne* is woman; *oikos* is of the ear; *lobos*, the lobe; *masso*, chew; and *philos*, loving. We include it here to show what could happen if there is a liberal free-for-all in Singlish.

There are other publications which contain such wild abortions and crossbreeds of English.

Sniglets by Rich Hall and Friends (Collier Macmillan Books) is one. Sniglets have been described as detritus of contemporary culture. Two examples of sniglets are:

niz, noun, an annoying hair on top of a movie screen; and

rolavert, noun, the system whereby one dog can quickly establish an entire neighbourhood network of barking.

The Devil's Dictionary by Ambrose Bierce (Stemmer House, Canada) is another. It contains such definitions as

bore, a person who talks to you when you wish him or her to listen;

patience, a minor form of despair, disguised as a virtue; and

rubuncles, noun, the bumps on an uncooked chicken.
It also contains poems by poets with the most unlikely names, for example,

Spring beckons! All things to the call respond:
The trees are leaving and the cashiers abscond.
—*Phela Orm*

H

had There is a painfully common misuse of *had*, many people believing it necessary to include *had* as a prefix for the past tense.

Where a report should have stated *The Board approved ...*, it is often reported as *The Board had approved ...*

More examples:
Singapore continues to use English even after the British had given us independence.
I had read that book.

hammer *I hammer you!* is a threat to beat you up. A corresponding word almost equivalent to *hammer* is *whack*.

hang him *Forget him*, as in
"Why Eggar so late?"
"Hang him; we'll go first."
It does not imply lynching.

The last *b* of a word is often not sounded clearly in Singlish, but *b* is sometimes accentuated too strongly. See *lamber*.

har-low Usually drawled by the lower end of that occupation that kills or stimulates business: the telephone operator. And while we are on this subject, it may be worth commenting on the fact that thousands of Singaporeans pick up the telephone with a grunt, a *yah!* or a toneless *harlow*.

In spite of all the courses organised for telephone courtesy and the advice given in the *Singapore Phone Book* Singaporeans very seldom identify themselves or their companies on the phone. This is true from senior executives to clerks and telephone operators. A few use the pompous *Mister* in front of their names. Another odd recent practice is to give only their first names, as though they don't want to reveal themselves fully to the stranger on the other end of the line. In answer to "Who am I talking to?" you will get a "Mary" or "Thomas". Even when "Mary what?" is asked you do not get an immediate reply. We have found it is better to ask the direct question, "What is your surname?"

If you hear a shout at your door, "Harlow postman," Toh Paik Choo (ref. 20) tells us that it is not someone calling out to the postman. *Harlow* precedes the Singapore postman's (or meter-reader's) announcement of his arrival. Ingenious!

hart *Doan gimme a hart time lah!* Not an unromantic refusal. Other derivations are:
Hart-working: She really put her soul into the job? She's a dear!
Hartware: Not the soft stuff in the heart of the computer but cold steel and plastic physical ware.

has Errors in the usage of *has* are very common. *The students all has to study history of music. We will not allow articles which has a critical slant on Singapore.*

having One common Singlish feature is misuse of the continuous tense:
I am having a gastric ulcer.
The job I'm having gives me good satisfaction.
I'm having a family business.

> A recent study by Newman (1986) in some primary schools in Singapore showed that of the formal areas of the language taught in Singapore schools, pronunciation was the one most neglected. —J. Foley (ref. 6)

he *He* and *she* get horribly intermixed in Singapore – in Singlish, not socially. Crewe (ref. 5) gives one example: "My sister never takes any money with him." (Note that this is an example of the wrong use of *him*, not the confusion of *with* and *from*.) Crewe has another: "He asked the woman in the next house whether he could lend them a dollar." (Funny how we seem to find examples involving money.)

It is a great pity that the clarity of the English *he* and *she* is not fully exploited. In many Asian languages, Chinese, Malay and Japanese for example, one is sometimes not sure which sex is doing what to whom. In "Varieties of English around the world – Singapore and Malaysia" (ref. 15), the error of pronoun copying is pointed out: "My husband he always like to gamble."

headmaster This word is not used in Singapore. *Principal* is used in its place without exception. Is it because the Ministry of Education feels that the female version may have connotations of old world Chinese concubines and the power of the head concubine?

heaps *Wah! Look at her heaps man!*
Lower your eyes, man; he meant *hips*.

heaty A Singlish adjective used to describe various foods or body conditions indicating a high level of a sort of metaphysical energy. This is based on ancient Chinese concepts of physiological heat but still plays a major role in the lives of Singapore Chinese. Durians and dog meat are *heaty*; *pisang hijau* (green bananas) and barley are *cooling*.

helpt Salesgirls keep offering us a mysterious service: *Can I helpt you?* We'll take up the offer one day. Be prepared to cope with variations such as *hepchoo*. Gesundheit!

herpes At a dinner, some doctors from overseas were startled when the waitress suggested we order *chicken with herpes*. A quick reference to the printed menu calmed their worst fears. It was chicken with *herbs*. Not a common mispronunciation, but one we thought which deserved some mention.

hole-on This is not an exhortation to keep digging. Nor is it some kind of golfer's cryptic expression. It is a telephone operator's standard phrase.

There is a variation, which may sound more imperative and rude but is not meant to be. It is *You hole-on!* At least it makes

Hole on!

it clear that she is not the one who is going to *hole-on*. There is another variation: *Hole-on the line* ... which has nothing to do with angling.

homemade prawns Good stuff it was in spite of our feeling of doubt about its natural origin when we saw it on a posh restaurant menu. Notice that in the true Singlish style we said *good stuff* first?

homogeneous The first syllable should be as in *Tom* (*BBC Guide*, ref. 3), not as in *home*.

hopefully We mention this word because the *BBC Guide* (ref. 3) states that it is one of the words purists guard with fanaticism. The objections are to the use of *hopefully* in contexts such as *Hopefully they will be available in the autumn.* It is often used like this in Singlish.
Thankfully can be used in an equally objectionable way, as in *Thankfully, the weather was fine. Reportedly* and *importantly* are two other words that grate on our conservative ears. The new Wordstar program, which not only corrects spelling but also brings one's notice to English that is odd, flags the word *importantly*.

hopeless We quote Tongue (ref. 21): "This is a very frequent adjective in the speech of ESM (English of Singapore and Malaysia) speaking university students and is used in a rather special way. Such statements as 'You're a hopeless case' and 'Hopeless lah, you' are normally uttered with affection and suggest that, whatever may be the inadequacies or shortcomings of the person addressed, the speaker finds them attractive, perhaps delightfully characteristic."

horn *Look out! She's backing into you. Horn her!*
It's back-seat drivers that bring out the beast in you.

hott Spoken with the accent on the *t*; almost hott–*er*. Has a specially apt application to really hot curries. Tongue (ref. 21) says that *hot-hot* is sometimes used for emphasis. This may be out of date now.

How On the phone, talking to a stranger: *How do you look like?* What should it be?

"What do you look like?" Rather rough.

"How do you look?" Vague.

"Tell me, how can I identify you?" Too precise.

"Will you have a carnation between your teeth?" Corny.

"Are you svelte and beautiful?" Shows your hand but it's a great time saver.

howboutyou A telescoped *How about you?* which seems to be used as a conversational return for a large variety of situations.

huff *Huff a loaf is better than none. Huff-past-six* was once used to describe something second-rate. Fading into disuse. *Huff-huff* seems to be preferred to *50-50*.

hurt *I hurt you are getting married.* Unhappy rejected suitor? The Singlish mispronunciation gives the old saying a kinder meaning: *Children should be seen and not hurt.*

I

I do awreddy I've done it.

I go first An announcement used for withdrawing politely. A direct translation from the Malay *Saya pergi dahulu* (*dulu*, in spoken Malay)? Falling into disuse.

I no mood Grammar: *I'm not in the mood.* Content: The correct thing to do is not to give in to your lethargic feelings and do what your mother, mother-in-law, boss, wife or even husband wants.

idea-r-of This *r* sound coming in between *idea* and *of* is an error that occurs all over the world, not only in Singapore. The *BBC Guide* (ref. 3) calls it *the intrusive r*. It also tends to pop up in *drawing* (drawring) and *law-abiding* (law-r-abiding).

idle king One who is extremely lazy; NS term. Beautifully expressive!

impots Movements of goods complementary to expots.

incharge Used in place of *manage* or *supervise*, as verb or noun. *I was incharge of all Katong area sales. He was the incharge.*

infeeneete *Infinite* is pronounced in'fi-nit; and *infinitive*, in-fin'i-tiv. On the split infinitive, the *BBC Guide* (ref. 3) says, "Infinitives have been split since at least the fourteenth century, and will continue to be split as time goes on, either for humorous effect (*Ross wants you to for God's sake stop attributing human behaviour to dogs.* —James Thurber), or because of the awkwardness that can result from writing some sentences with unsevered infinitives."

inform In recent years Singaporeans have started using *inform* without an object: *He informed that the standard of English was deteriorating.* Inform is also very often mishandled by dropping the *-ed*: *Please be inform that …*

introduce Fairly common. When some boys are talking about one of their sisters, someone will interject, "Why never introduce?" The economy of breath principle.

involve A common error:
"What kind of work you involve?"
"I involve in the design of …"

IOU Singaporeans handle this abbreviation with the ease and confidence with which they handle all abbreviations they create, but little do they realise that IOU has changed over the years as the English language has changed. The letters IOU originally stood for *I owe unto …*

irregardless As in *Let's press on, irregardless* – a Singlish original. *Irregardless* is not in the English dictionary. We are willing to bet that this statement will be challenged if you make it in company.

is The verb *to be* is a great stumbling block in Singapore: *During the period of probation which he has just completed he is attached to ...*

As is mentioned on page ... The inability to use the verb *to be* is indeed a serious matter because *is* is one of the ten words that occur most frequently. The other nine are: *the*, *of*, *and*, *to*, *a*, *in*, *that*, *it*, and of course, since we are all human, *I*.

is it? Used incessantly for *Is that so?* Apart from being used as a comment or response in dialogue, the phrase is sometimes used to frame a question: *Is it your working place is near your house? So you find it interesting, is it?*

is narting Used as *Don't mention it* in response to *Thank you*. Synonyms are *Small matter* or *Narting much lah*.

isn't The use of *Isn't* as a call for sympathetic agreement or comment – as in *Isn't it ghastly!* or *Isn't she awfully fat?* – hardly ever occurs in conversation in Singapore. But Singaporeans constantly use *isn't it?* or its telescoped form *innit* to turn a statement into a question: *National day is next week, isn't it?* Not unlike the English *ain't it?* Some Indians do this tag-question trick with the word *ne?* A variation heard at times in Singlish is *no?* at the end of a statement. It has been suggested to us that teachers tend to use this tag question as a method of inviting feedback.

J

Jahg-goo-are The beast and the car.

janerally Generally. At all times, not just in January.

Jappanese Pronounced with the accent on *pan* and not in the least likely to have derived from the verb meaning to lay a hard varnish or to lacquer a surface.

jeero Zero.

jelak The Malay word which has no equivalent in English. We hazard a translation: *a feeling of fullness and opulent sufficiency.*

> Sociolinguistic interest in English in Singapore goes back to 1974, the year Tongue's *The English of Singapore and Malaysia* was published. Since then, articles and books have appeared on the subject with increasing regularity – which have had the effect of raising important empirical research questions. On the other hand, a common problem with all these studies is their lack of methodological controls on data collection. —Anderson (1985) Quoted in ref. 6, p. xiv

Jones, Daniel This man wrote a book of mammoth significance to the English language, and the clarification of sounds he established made the birth of Singlish possible. *The English Pronouncing Dictionary* is the Bible of certain sects of the tribe of linguistics wallahs. It is the reference work *par excellence*. Although it was first published in 1917 it is still being reprinted.

If one decides to throw oneself fully into the cause of abolition of Singlish this is an essential weapon. It shows how the sounds of English come from different parts of the mouth and throat, for example how the tongue should be higher for *u* than for *a*, points out that the English have difficulty understanding American pronunciations while Americans from Texas to Alabama understand RP with comparative ease, informs you to your surprise that *Batho* is a first name which can be pronounced in two ways, and gives you the confidence of being able to say *Eryx* and *Iliffe* perfectly. We keep it on our bedside table. It never fails us. Many a night when we have tossed in bed struggling with Singlish problems, or lain insomniac about chicken-or-egg causal sequences, or wondered if we switched off the air-con at the office, it has within three minutes put us at peace in deep restful slumber. Whether you're a linguistics nut or a layman, you need a Daniel Jones.

Jurong Industrial Quite often Singaporeans cut off the final word *Estate*. We think it is an admirable economy of words. At least it is words; not abbreviations. Similar lopped off area names are:

I work at Shenton: *Way* is left out.

… the first bus stop after Eunos: *Jalan* Eunos

Katong Shopping: Katong Shopping *Centre*

just Singlish has a special use in the phrase, *You mean you only just know about your husband and …*

K

kachauration Although this hybrid noun is not being used very often we include it as an example of a Singlish creation. The Malay word *kachau* (now spelt *kacau*) means to disturb, to irritate, annoy. So *kachauration* means a great botheration.

kaki *Leg* in Malay. Often used in Singlish to mean *friends*, or *the gang*. *Kaki* is also used in the context of games partners, as in *mahjong kaki*.

kampong It means *village* but is nowadays applied in the sense of the backwoods. *Kampong* is used in South African English. The Indonesians whom the Dutch moved to South Africa in the colonial days gave a few words to the South African variety of English.

kaypoh Nosey. From Hokkien.

keep *Keep* is often used as a Singlish substitution of *put away*: *Keep your toys, girl*. We pondered about this and wondered if when a Singaporean says he was going to keep a woman, he really means *put away*. A variation is *keep-by*. Rare.

kiasu Afraid of failure. From Hokkien.

kiln Pronounced as though they are *killin'* the word. Singlish speakers find *kiln* as difficult as *film* – or as difficult as westerners find the Chinese *Ng*.

kine Nothing at all to do with the *kine* which is to cows as swine is to hogs. *He's a very kine ole man.*

kunchi *Kunchi* (*kunci* in the modern spelling) is key in Malay. The word was used quite a lot in 'early Singlish', but is seldom used now. We mention it firstly to make the point that as English education spread, fewer Malay words were intermixed with English in verbal communication, and secondly to use *kunchi* as a warning to new expatriate arrivals that they should not try to use Chinese or Malay words unless they are sure they have mastered their pronunciation.

Charles Allen relates an anecdote in his book that will emphasise our advice. It is about a newly arrived colonial civil servant talking to his servant.

"Guy tried very hard to teach me the basic words to say to the servants and I used to repeat them religiously every evening. I got my accent more or less right but the time came when he had to be away overnight. I was rather nervous but he said, 'You will be quite all right with Ah Chi. All you have to do is to tell him to lock everything that will lock,' and he told me what to say which I, faithfully, thought I knew well. So when Ah Chi came into the room and said goodnight, I said, 'You must kenching sini, kenching sana, kenching sini, kenching sana,' and I went on saying this to Ah Chi, whose face never altered. He didn't let on by any indication at all that I was saying something wrong and off he went, back to his quarters, which are always at the back of a bungalow in Malaya and eventually I heard him laughing hysterically, and his family all laughing and laughing, and I thought, 'That's funny, why are they laughing?' So when Guy came home he said 'How have you been?' And I said 'Oh, I was all right, but when I told Ah Chi kenching sini, kenching sana, they just roared with laughter.' And then, of course, Guy roared with laughter. What I should have been saying was 'kunchi' which means lock, but what I was saying was 'kenching sini, kenching sana', which means 'pee here, pee there', so no wonder they laughed."

kwei-loh Literally, devil fellow – foreigner. It is interesting to note that whereas the Chinese and Japanese had depreciating terms for foreigners, the Malays did not. They used the straight description of *orang puteh* (white man) and later the fairly bland term *Mat Salleh*. Both the Japanese and Chinese use unemotive descriptive expressions these days; the Japanese call them *gaijin* (outside people) and the Chinese call them *ta pi tsu* (the big-nosed ones).

L

lady Used in Singlish where the English would refer to a person cautiously with *woman*, to avoid any status judgements and to ensure that no humiliating implications are conveyed, much in the same vein as public toilets are labelled *Gentlemen* all over the world, without discrimination of the user's conduct and breeding. New arrivals in Singapore find this confusing and amusing.

We see one supermarket labels its pack of ten or twelve okra *lady finger*. This is quite unacceptable. Our feminists will accept nothing but *person's fingers*.

Lairssons Lessons, not affairs with cute teachers.

lamber As in *Mary had a little lamber*. Whether Mary was the ewe who had the little lamb, whether she had lamb with mint sauce, or whether she only had a little because she had to watch her cholesterol, in Singlish she had a little *lamber*.

language We asked a Singaporean how well he spoke Bahasa Malaysia. His answer struck us as odd at first, but later we thought it very creative and wondered if the English faculty wordlords would consider this poetic Singlish. "I cannot work with it, but I can live in it."

latchstring R.K. Tongue (ref. 21) points out that clusters of consonants give the Singapore tongue pronunciation problems. *Film* and *milk* are two examples. We tried *latchstring* on our friends and they passed with flying colours. We believe this word with its six consonants in a row may be the largest consonant cluster in the English language.

late This expression mentioned in *Lagi Goondu* (ref. 20) may be one of the first Singapore-created proverbs: *Late is late oraidy*. We reckon that's in the same class as Dale Carnegie's brilliant *Don't saw sawdust*.

leaf *I'm on leaf now*. Fanatic vegetarian on holiday?

leeaship The lazy tongue on *leadership*.

leefs "He keeps trying to kees me in the leefs."
"How romantic! Kisses in the arbour!"
"The HDB leefs lah!"

lef Overheard in a department store:
"I'll take two."
"But then I lef one only."
She didn't mean she had a left-handed one only.
She meant, "I have only one left."

> What does a Singaporean mean by *next Monday*?
> See *next Monday*.

less Sometimes *less* and *fewer* are confused in Singlish. We quote Theodore Bernstein: "The general rule is to use less for quantity and fewer for number."

let-fly To explode in anger and pour out one's wrath verbally. Becoming obsolete.

liaison A liaison, socially acceptable or otherwise, is wrongly pronounced with the stress on *lie* in Singlish. Don't get the wrong end of a description of administrative consultancy: *He lies with her regularly.*

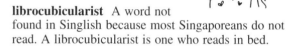

librocubicularist A word not found in Singlish because most Singaporeans do not read. A librocubicularist is one who reads in bed.

liebree A slipshod *library*. Usually staffed by *libarians*. Did you know that at some stage in their varied careers Pope Pious XI, Mao Tse-tung and Casanova were all librarians? (Ref. 9)

lier A mispronunciation of *lawyer*. Rare, with no defamatory implications intended. The Indians have the strongest tendency to mis-mouth this in spite of being, in our opinion, the greatest linguists in the world.

lifestyle A much used word in Singapore. It has been so overworked all over the world that *The Economist Pocket Style Book* states clearly: "Prefer WAY OF LIFE."

like Besides being overused, there is a common propensity to add *like* unnecessarily to the end of some sentences: *I like to know how your new girl frien' looks like.* An expressive exclamation which is quite common is *Like real!* The use of *like* is changing in the world outside Singapore. We quote from the *BBC Guide* (ref. 3) and include the footnote.

"Grammarians used to instruct readers never to use 'like' as a conjunction, except in a few humorous expressions (e.g. 'like the man said', 'If you knew Susie like I know Susie'), but modern writers regularly use this construction, especially when the verb is repeated in the same sentence: 'Some girls change their lovers like they change their winter clothes.' (Graham Greene) ...

"Footnote: And other writers; Evelyn Waugh, commenting on Henry Green's *Pack My Bag* (1940), remarked, 'Only one thing disconcerted me ... The proletarian grammar – the likes for asses, the bikes for bicycles, etc ...'"

limerick Not used very often, but when it is, Singlish speakers put the accent on the second syllable. It should be on the first. If you do not know what a limerick is, we give you two samples.

> There was a girl from Singapore,
> Who had a meal at Gerrard Street,
> "Hey Honkie your meat
> is too hart to eat."
> They cursed her and called her a whore.

> There was a man from south Johor,
> whose English was quite impure,
> said the speech therapis',
> "I can only say this,
> you live too close to Singapore."

line A telephonist's stock phrase when a female you are trying to reach is engaged talking to another on the phone – *She's on the line* – even in the most respectable of establishments.

Another variation: *May I know who is calling on the line?*

> **Spitting is a filthy habit, and we are slowly but surely eradicating it in Singapore. Are we? See *speet*.**

long time no see This is the paragon of pidgin; it was used a lot in Malaysia and Singapore before 1960 or so but is slowly disappearing as a hackneyed jocose opener. It reminds us of a painfully corny boy-scout campfire skit. Those were the days when television had not shattered the simple honest enjoyment of raw puns and kampung slapstick and before it had exposed the mediocrity of campfire humour that brought laughter till one's belly ached, innocent of the low theatrical quality of it all. It went like this:

A table by the campfire. An elderly man sits at the table. Enter an equally elderly man.
AH KOW: Wei! Ah Beng ah!
AH BENG: Wei! Ah Kow! Long time no see ah.
AH KOW: Why no come to see me?
AH BENG: Velly busy ah. Long see no time.
The two men mumble a conversation, then ...
AH BENG: Long no see time (*pointing to the adjacent room wall at an imaginary clock*).
Exit Ah Beng.
AH KOW: See time no long ... (pause) ... (chuckles) Ah Beng! Rong time no see lah!
Exit Ah Kow.

luggages A common error. Tongue (ref. 21) reports the opposite error: "All the lady prizewinners were given a luggage." *Baggage* is given the same mishandling: "Song Guan never flies with more than one baggage and he always carries a sketch and description of it, including a complete and detailed list of its contents, in case he has to fill in a lost-baggages form. He says Murphy was an optimist." *Baggage* is a collective noun and has no plural. Neither can one say *one baggage*. Note that the definition of baggage includes things like tents and golf clubs and that department of consolation in every airport could be called *Lost Baggage*. Perhaps *Lost Luggage* is preferred worldwide because it alliterates. God alone knows if the fatigue-dazed traveller, staggering up to the counter, fuming with rage at the sickening inefficiency of the airline, resolving on the spur of the moment never to fly with them again, no matter what carnal promises the TV ad. suggests, will be soothed by the alliterative nicety of *Lost Luggage*.

A much travelled friend pointed out to us that only at Heathrow are the signs correct; they say *Baggage Reclaim*. Is he right? What is the difference between luggage and baggage? Luggage is what the British used. Baggage is American. At one time the British used *baggage* when travelling by sea or air and *luggage* for travel on land.

Is Singlish a pidgin English? See *Pidgin*.

lurve Absolute mutilation of *love*. When slobbered out with intense passion in *I lurrrve you*, it is particularly nauseating. Crewe (ref. 5) gives an example illustrating a four-letter word error with a sentence that makes one pause: "Love is simply a four-lettered word in spite of its implied difference."

lusstime Whether mispronounced or not, *last time* is often used in place of *previously*: *Last time we only needed two copies.*

M

M-16 Michael Chiang in *Army Daze* says that the NS recruit is told he must treat his M-16 like his wife and he is then made to sleep with her, strip her and put her together again in the dark and oil her. It makes us wonder if thousands of our young men have not reacted subconsciously in a perverse and converse way and treated their wives as a mere offensive article.

mahmee This could mean either the Chinese noodle dish or *mummy*. But be careful of the word *mummy*. In the dim-lit world of Singapore nightclubs it has another meaning. If you hear an emotion-charged muttering, "I'd like to get that mummy into my arms," don't jump to the assumption that he is a necromaniac. *Mummy* is the Singlish for *madam* – in its full French meaning, the controller of the girls.

mail If an unmarried woman tells you, "I didn't receive a single mail this week," it has nothing to do with her social life with the opposite sex. It's merely the old singular/plural error; the very common failure to get to the meaning of collective nouns. In Singlish there is a singular mail.

makan The verb *to eat* or the noun *a meal*. *Makan angin*, the Malay phrase for *taking the air*, appeared in

Singlish conversation fairly frequently in the past but as fewer and fewer Singaporeans can speak Malay it is dying out. There are still living inhabitants who may even use the Indonesian *cuci mata* (pronounced *chuchi mata*, literally *wash the eyes*) for the ageless pastime of watching the girls go by.

malu Used in the sense of being embarrassed or shy. Actually Malay distinguishes between being ashamed and shy or hesitating with humiliation. They would not say *Don't be malu* when offering a second helping of food, for example, but would use the word *segan*.

mama A word from the Tamil language applied loosely to people and objects Indian. The most common usage is in *the mama shop*, which is found all over Singapore and Malaysia. The *mama* shops or stalls sell just about everything: cigarettes, matches, medicines, toys, trinkets, soap, toothpaste, toothbrushes, pens, paper, envelopes, needles, condoms (which we are advised should be used on every conceivable occasion) – the list is almost endless. They were almost a supermarket in a ten-foot frontage along the 'five-foot-ways' (pavements; sidewalks).

mammeries Heard in a nightclub:
Mammeries ... in the corners of my mind,
Faded water-coloured mammeries ...

manage The word appears sometimes in forms such as *I doan tink that I can manage to go on a bus with all those files*. It is sometimes mispronounced.

Another use of manage:

"How are things with you?"
"Not so bad ... Can manage lah."

Talking of just being able to manage and managing language we would like to inject a thought W.J. Crewe shared in his book (ref. 5). Should we not accept Singlish in everyday conversation and informal communication, and only strive to achieve Standard English in formal written communication? It spins off other questions. Don't the British themselves switch between their factory floor dialects and their boardroom dialects? Are the Chinese able to jump from one dialect to another so easily because they know both dialects well? Will the world understand our informal tongue? For example, will MFA (Ministry of Foreign Affairs) representatives convey the nuances of our diplomatic annoyance if they say "Why you worry!" or would the past Prime Minister of Britain have been ruffled if he had been addressed as Mr Airwood Heat?

Mandarin Real Singapore wit:
"I doan tink I'll have deener tonight. I'll just have two Mandarins."
"Turned cannibal eh?"

marinetime Singlish version of *maritime*. Conveys the meaning, anyway.

massahge Not only mispronounced but crammed with other undertones. Study the Yellow Pages.

master Often the adjectival use of the Master of Arts and similar academic degrees is not realised, as in "When I first applied for my Master …" This grammatical error, we hasten to add, was made by a scientist. But the *Straits Times* caption under a photograph of 26 July 1991, "Miss K, who will do a one year master …", is surely unforgivable for a newspaper.

matibaik *The New Paper* reported an amusing mix-up in a doctor's surgery in mid-September 1988. After examining the dear old lady and telling her that she was quite ill, she said to the doctor *matibaik*, which in Malay is literally *better to die*. The doctor, alarmed at her pessimism, hastened to tell her that it wasn't as bad as all that. But she kept saying *matibaik*. Eventually a nurse who spoke Singlish came to the rescue. The little old lady meant she wanted multi-vite.

mats Singaporeans are generally good at mats: pure mats, additional mats, applied mats.

meaningful It appears it is usually necessary to be precise and distinguish the true from the false in Singapore by qualifying all discussions as 'meaningful'.

med-dee-sin Tongue (ref. 1) mentions a possible Malaysian use of the mispronounced word only for the medicine that is shaken and taken, keeping the pronunciation intact for the studying of medicine. Probably a difference of usage of the word by different strata of society. The common man rarely has a need to mention medicine in a context outside what he has to consume or apply. The correct English pronunciation is however not what one would expect. It telescopes the sounds as Singlish tends to do, with med'sin.

meedyear Not some special year to enjoy the old English mead, but just the middle of the year. Neither does meadnight have a connection with the old drink.

meeshun Mission impossible to Singlish.

meetpoint Where the top and bottom, or left and right meet; in the meaty middle. A double error within one word, the *i* becoming *ee* and the *d* becoming a sound between *t* and *d*.

minutes Seen on a restaurant menu: *minutes steak*. Rare; in occurrence, but probably overdone at that place.

mischief The Singlish accent is on *chief* and it is pronounced *chief* in Singlish instead of *chif*.

more The rule with *more* seems to be, the more mores the merrier. Every comparison is accentuated with redundancies such as *more better*, *more rougher*, *more bigger* ... and even *more ideal*. The errors of redundant *mores* are understandable. Both the Malay and Chinese language have prefixes to convert adjectives into comparative adjectives. In both cases the *more* equivalent is a fairly strong sound and is often accented in conversation: *lagi* in Malay; *keng* in Chinese.

mosely *Cantonese are mosely they deal in some of these gosmith shops, you know ... an' Hakka orso gosmith.* (From Platt, Weber and Ho, ref. 15.)

much *Much* gets the full mutilation treatment in Singlish:
There are much tall shady trees in the Botanic Gardens.
I am very much impressed.
I will consider any job but probably not so much in the uniform groups.

mucketing Not straight honest-to-god *selling*, but mucketing. It must have been created by the sales people in their standing war against the *mar*keting types. The one we've heard that takes a hefty swipe at *mar*keting is:

New Personnel Officer: Can I call the marketing staff salespersons?

Sales Manager: Would you call a barnacle a ship?

mudder There may be some Freudian link with *udder* in this pronunciation distortion; in the same family of errors as *farder*, *grandfarder* and *brarder*.

mugging Explained in *Made in Singapore*, by Corrine Chia, K.K. Seet, and Pat M. Wong, as "In other parts of the world this activity is referred to as 'swotting'; 'mugging' is in fact uniquely Singaporean, and bears no relation to subterranean encounters in the New York subway."

muriel "We have a muriel on our school now."
"Oh. Is she nice?"
"Beautiful. It's beautiful."
"It?"
"Yes, Mr Wong, the art teacher, painted it."

music Any parent or teacher knows the tremendous influence of pop music on young people. John Honey (ref. 8) points out that it has been the main motivation for millions to learn English all over the world. In Britain today it is one of the major influences on accents and of American English. In the heyday of the Beatles the Liverpool variety of English known as Scouse "became fashionable ... but quickly passed and Scouse resumed its place among the most stigmatised accents" (ref. 8). Paul McCartney now has an accent barely distinguishable from RP. Does this make it imperative that we put our best speakers on all the music programmes on RCS?

must *Must be he missed the bus* means *He must have missed the bus.*

muzn't This is true-blue Singlish. As with many similar words, the *s* becomes a *z*. Actually this is a natural drift as the tongue slips so easily into the *z* sound after certain consonants. The Japanese accept this and change their *sushi* (vinegared rice with raw meat) with compound words like *sakezushi* (sushi with sake). That's worth trying.

my's one Mine. A real gem! Maybe we can auction it at Sotheby's. Frequently heard today are *my one* and *your one* instead of *mine* and *yours*. And, of course, *his one*, *her one* and *their one* follows.

What did Ezra Pound say about education? See *normal*.

myffs Myths of Singlish. Akin to boff (both).

myself *Myself* is used very often in various ways: *Myself, I took up computer clubs.*

N

names British names are often painfully distorted by Singaporeans. We will not list these funny distortions to spare the feelings of any Cholomondeley or Ruthvern who may be reading this. We will only list a few names, selected from Fowler (ref. 20), to help Singaporeans frustrated with the apparent disregard for conventional pronunciation guidelines when it comes to mouthing British names.

Beauchamp *is pronounced*	Becham
Beaulieu	Buli
Blount	Blunt
Broke	Brook
Cherwell	Charwell
Cholomondeley	Chumli
Cowper	Cooper
Harewood	Harwood
Home	Hum
Ker	Kar
Keyenes	Kanz
Marjoribanks	Marchbanks
Ruthvern	Riven
Sandys	Sandz
Worburn	Woobun

narting *Nothing* in Singlish. A probable conversation illustrates this:
"What did you do in NS?"
"Narting lah."
"Arh?"
"Yes lah. I deed narting lah!"
"You mean every day you deed narting?"
"Yah man! Narting."
"But you got promoted to sergeant?"
"Yes lah. Because I deed narting."
"Ha?"
"I tell you man, I deed narting. So no gabra. So I got promotion."
"Oh like dat ah?"
"Yah, like dat."

neck to neck Neck *and* neck is the true English form. Actually, *neck to neck* seems more appropriate to us.

needil The cluster of consonant-sounds problem. Get your quotation right if you're going to say that bit from the Bible. Don't mix them up as the comedian Johnny Speight deliberately did at a Royal Variety Performance in 1972: "'Cos as the Lord Jesus said, it will be easier for a needle to pass through the eye of a camel than for a rich man to enter the Kingdom of Heaven." (Ref. 4)

negative examples We quote in full a list of 26 sentences of advice to Japanese writers from the book *Kagaku Eibun Giho—The Art of Scientific Writing in English* (Shin'ichi Hyodo, University of Tokyo Press, 1986). It punches home each point by stating it incorrectly. Those who want to move their Singlish up to English may find the tips useful.

1. Make sure each pronoun agrees with their antecedent.
2. Just between you and I, the case of pronouns is important.
3. Watch out for irregular verbs which have crope into English.
4. Verbs has to agree in number with their subjects.
5. Don't use no double negatives.
6. Being bad grammar, a writer should not use dangling modifiers.
7. Join clauses good like a conjunction should.
8. A writer must not shift your point of view.
9. About sentence fragments.
10. Don't use run-on sentences you have to punctuate them.
11. In letters essays and reports use commas to separate items in series.
12. Don't use commas, which are not necessary.
13. Parenthetical words however should be enclosed in commas.
14. Its important to use apostrophes properly in everybodys writing.
15. Don't abbrev.
16. Check to see if any words out.
17. In the case of a report check to see that jargon-wise, it's A-O.K.
18. As far as incomplete constructions, they are wrong.
19. About repetition, the repetition of a word might be real effective repetition—take, for instance, the repetition of Abraham Lincoln.

20. In my opinion, I think that an author when he is writing should definitely not get into the habit of making use of too many unnecessary words that he does not really need in order to put his message across.
21. Use parallel construction not only to be concise but also to clarify.
22. It behooves us all to avoid archaic expressions.
23. Mixed metaphors are a pain in the neck and ought to be weeded out.
24. Consult a dictionary to avoid mispellings.
25. To ignorantly split an infinitive is a practice to religiously avoid.
26. Last but not least, lay off clichés.

never happen A much used abbreviation. It is used either in the context of predicting the future or making sudden promises. Two examples:

"When you grow up and marry a rich man with a Mercedes-Benz …"
"Never happen lah!"

"Cherry (this is a loving middle-class wife speaking to her husband, adding romantic French words to her repertoire of affectionate terms), if you go to Patpong when you are in Bangkok, I'll keel you."
"Never happen lah!"

We are not sure if *never!* by itself is an abbreviation of *never happen!* or an independent entity by itself created many years earlier. Tongue (ref. 21) gives an example:

"You took my pen?"
"Never!"

next door A common error – now corrected, we think – used to be, *Park next door to that tree.* Perhaps if he had said *next door to that car* he would have been right?

next Monday (or Tuesday, Wednesday, etc.) One has to be extremely careful in Singapore because there are many who do not follow the British practice of calling the first Monday coming up *next Monday* and the one after that *Monday week*. In Singapore the words *this Monday* and *next Monday* have no clear generally accepted meanings. Our all-organising authorities did a tremendous job straightening out the *storey* and *floor* conflict in vertical space. Surely some authority can standardise these definitions of time?

nice-nice Middle-aged woman in a department store: "Haven't you got anything with those nice-nice frills?" A *nice-nice* Singlish expression going out of use.

nineteen-nought-belum A date that will never come. *Belum* is *not yet* in Malay. Falling into disuse.

no idea A favourite Singlish response of telephone operators.
"Where is Mr Steef (Steve) Tan?"
"No idea."
"When will he be back?"
"No idea."
"Where has he gone?"
"No idea."

no sweat A favourite phrase, which has been losing out to *no problem*.

**Aren't teachers a key factor in improving Singlish?
See *pro-noun-see-a-tion*.**

noh This has nothing at all to do with that strange form of Japanese theatre in which people say the oddest things, in the weirdest tone of voice, while moving around the stage aimlessly, and the musicians at the back carry on with their thing with great gusto. It is the Singlish *no*.

The diphthong of the English *o* has not yet been discovered by the average Singaporean. Anyway, whether it is pronounced in the proper RP style or as the Japanese noh play, it is still the best method of birth control.

Tongue points out that there are eight diphthongs in the English language; together with 24 consonants and 12 vowels they add up to 44 sounds. And all this is written with 26 letters of the alphabet. The *Oxford Paperback* lists 56.

There is one interesting fact in the comparison of the English language with Chinese. A British linguistics man woke up to it about ten years ago. The English dictionary lists English words in writing. There are 26 groups: the letters of the alphabet. If one decided to classify them by sound a number running to thousands will have to be listed. Listing Chinese by the written form presents horrible problems of numbers. But listing them by sounds reduces the classification groups to less than a hundred. He devised a computer system to access Chinese words and phrases by sound. It is a brilliant piece of software.

nor-chet Not yet.

normal This euphemistic adjective is applied to the slow learners in Singapore; and it's not a dropping of the *sub* prefix. The normal or average pupils are in the express stream. And unexpectedly, appropriately, the schools for the nose-to-the-grindstone students are known as the SAP schools.

Many believe that education in Singapore is organised for the cream and not the mass; for the tail of that Gaussian curve and not the huge hump. Ezra Pound would agree with such a policy. He wrote, "Real education must ultimately be limited to men who insist on knowing; the rest is mere sheep herding." (Ref. 4)

normally A rare and strange use of the adverb: "Which JC are you normally from?" (We must explain that JC means Junior College and the girl being questioned only went to one JC. Our system doesn't allow one to keep moving around anyway.)

Normally is used very often. "What sports do you normally play?"

Singlish is not the only extra-Britain dialect of English that struggles with *normally*. Japlish too has its difficult encounters with the applications of *normally*. A SWET (Society of Writers, Editors and Translators – yes, writers and editors do meet each other, smiling sometimes…) newsletter (October 1987) takes a stab at the Japlish use of *normally*: "He eats apples normally."

If a sentence starts with *He normally eats apples for breakfast*, we expect it to end with some such information as, *but when he has a hangover, he eats pomegranates instead.* If, on the other hand, the sentence starts with *He eats apples normally for breakfast*, the expected end is along the lines of, *but at lunch he mashes them with soy sauce.*

norvel A rather rare pronunciation of *novel*, over-rounding the *r*. Philip Larkin, the poet, once said about novels, "Far too many relied on the classic formula, a beginning, a muddle and an end."

not Interfering foreigner: "Are you not going too far in restricting the freedom of your people?"
Singaporean: "Yes! We all realise that freedom to preach communism and that sort of thing can destroy a nation."

Singlish, like Japlish, refuses to cope with the totally illogical response form to the English negative question. It is absurd to suggest to any Asian that the answer to the question, "Is there no Monopolies Commission in Singapore?" should be answered with a *Yes*, because it's *No!* There's no such thing here. This is the capitalists' paradise. For Heaven's sake, Mammon is God.

not enough Used as *moreover, on top of all that*, etc.: *Not enough, she wants to drink the most expensive cocktail on the menu.*

not exactly Used without error in language, but frequently employed with the same evasiveness as the *yes-and-no* answer which the civil service loves so dearly. In the same woolly strain the phrases *about, roughly* and *not really* occur quite often. *About, roughly twenty* is a typical Singlish redundancy. But isn't this a universal human trait?

not shy Forward, brash, precocious. *She not shy one* describes a brazen woman. See **one**.

nutes *Nudes* not fully rounded off. There's an account of the witty Kaufman meeting unexpectedly a nude eccentric producer in his office. Without batting an eyelid, he said, "Excuse me, Sir, your fly is open."

O

odd An odd plural error: *How many? Tirty odds.* Singlish speakers just love the use of *odd* when they are not sure: *We met ten odd women that night.*

offer If you see this on a sign it means *special offer*. One of the odd Singlish shortenings. In other parts of the world the abbreviation for special offer is *specials*.

official This adjective hits a high in frequency of occurrence in Singapore. It might make the Guinness list one day. Everybody, not just civil servants, waits for a chance to slip it in. Crewe (ref. 5), writing in 1977 before *the* disease hit the world, gives an example: "Any aids sent to this organisation will be properly recorded in our official records." Should we assume that somewhere in the archives of the stricken organisation there are tomes of improper contagious *un*official records? We came across one *official* slip; but this sort of mix-up is rare: "The ribbon was officiously cut by..." It does go to some people's heads when they are asked to cut a ribbon...or tie a knot for that matter ...

OK There is a special Singapore way of pronouncing this which is heard fairly often in middle-class circles. There is a touch of *h* in the monosyllabic *o* and just the faintest suggestion of the Australian *kai* in the *k*. We find it charming.

ole Perhaps this swallowing of the *d* end of *old* is universal: *Ole Man River*, *the good ole days* … but at times it is really slurred over in Singlish:
"How-oo-arr-you?"
"I'm OK; so-so lah."
"Come again?"
"I'm fine."
(Once more, with feeling.) "I asked: how-*ole*-are-*you*?"

omelette Pronounced the way it is spelt. It's the first *e* that shouldn't be there; *om-eh-leht* is the Singlish way, and *omm-leht* the RP way.

on *Please on the switch.* There is the parallel *off*. We have never encountered this in other forms such as *I have onn-ed the light* or *This switch cannot be off-ed.*

one Besides signifying possession (see **my's one**), *one*, like lah, is used to round off a sentence: *She not shy one*, *Doan be like dat one*, *How can one*?

or not Very common, and easy to slip into if you hear it often enough: *You wan' to go or not? Can or not?*

own *You should be able to stand on your own two feet.* Probably comes from the Chinese, which has no nouns like feet that parallel the English plural. Singaporeans just cannot use the English expression *stand on your own feet* without specifying the number.

P

panter The animal, not the jogger.

panthouse A pad where the middle-aged who can afford it gasp for air in the peaks of their pleasure.

parts *I am actually taking parts in Community Centre activities.* Whether you are holding your breath at the crack of dawn and making sloth-slow movements with the Tai Chi group every morning, dashing round a table hitting a little ball while pouring with perspiration in the evenings, blowing till your face is red through a trumpet on Wednesdays, tying knots in macrame classes on Thursdays, slicing garlic and the tips of your fingers into thin slivers, pounding cardamoms, fennel, cummin seeds, chillies, ginger and frying the whole mess up with fellow cooking fanatics on Fridays, shouting *doh-see-doh*, clapping your hands, jumping around like a kangaroo on Saturdays, and hurling yourself into the Sunday picnics with utter enthusiasm at East Coast

Parkway, including belting out *Chan-mali-chan* lustily, you have to envelope the total description of your activities with the Community Centre groups, with the singular *PART*. You can expand on it after your opening statement, but that has to be "I take part in Community Centre activities" if you want to speak proper English.

Incidentally, what do you do on Mondays and Tuesdays? Have you thought of reading a book in English to improve your EL1 on Mondays? No? Ahhh ... of course, you're Singaporean. You don't read. But there will be people who will defend your dislike of reading. Anthony Powell may be one. He wrote in *The Kindly Ones* about someone who did not read:

"He took no pleasure in reading. No doubt that was a wise precaution for a man of action, whose imagination must be rigorously disciplined if the will is to be unsapped by daydreams, painting and music being, for some reason, less deleterious than writing in that respect."

Something wrong with that sentence construction? Oh well, even the great slip.

passed Singaporeans generally use this verb correctly, but we did encounter a rare use on a building site that is worth relating.

The foreman, his face grim, informed us:

"Mr Chonomuthu passed last night."

"He came this way last night?"

"No sir, he passed last night. The funeral is tomorrow."

We thought that this was an odd omission of *away*, but in Canada one says so-and-so has *passed*.

patrol Do not be alarmed if someone who is giving you a lift says he has to stop and get *patrol*. He's not going to cram the car with a bunch of national servicemen. It's just the local brand of *petrol*.

penalty Singlish puts the accent on the second syllable incorrectly. And Singlish sounds the second syllable with something like *nall*.

personal Very common: *For my own personal interest.*

perusal One of the unnecessary words that Singlish teems with in the written form. Internal memos add to the bytes load with *for your perusal* and *for your necessary action* in offices all over the city. We came across one startling appearance of *perusal* in a job application letter, which still puzzles us: "I would like to submit my short perusal for your consideration."

pick If a woman tells you that she has to pick her daughter at five o'clock, it doesn't mean that she is going to an adoption agency or is going home to pick the nits out of her daughter's hair. She means she is going to *pick her up*.
The converse expression is *pick me back*, meaning *pick me up and take me home*.

It is interesting to note that the Zulu language gives rise to a parallel twist of the verb *to pick*. In Zulu the same word is used for *pick* and *scoop*, and Zulus will talk of *scooping* flowers from the fields in English.

I have to pick my daughter. . . .

pidgin English Someone said to us that Singlish is a type of pidgin English and we really got all het up about it. It is emphatically *not* a pidgin. She quoted the Chambers definition of pidgin as "any jargon consisting of English and another language", and added that as soon as a Singaporean says "I've got two jambu trees in my garden", he's speaking pidgin. Incensed, we rushed to the same Chambers. *Jargon* is described as "chatter, twittering: confused talk: slang: artificial or barbarous language [that really got to us]: the terminology of a profession, art group, etc." And by chance we found *jambu* in the same English dictionary. We swung into the attack.

Singlish is definitely not a pidgin. It is the English language with the sound of the Malay and Chinese tongues; it has the fundamental form and structures of the English language with a few aberrations of grammar and often with improvements to its parent with such expressions as *finished awreddy* and *I ever been to Frisco*.

We reminded her that the word *pidgin* came from the China Chinese mumbling of *business English* that got itself quite confused with the bird word *pigeon*, giving rise to *It's not my pigeon*. It is a corruption, not a melding or a clone. Singlish for all its faults is unique.

That was on 7 September 1988. We remember the date because the next morning, having cooled down after a good night's sleep, we read in the *Straits Times* that a high priest of the language from Leeds, Dr Loreto Todd, had exalted the pidgin of The Cameroons and Papua New Guinea (Tok Pisin) to the status of a proper language: "… simpler, yes, but definitely not inferior to English," she said. We do not dispute the utility of pidgins, but just listen to the Cameroon pidgin: *Singapore fain pass mark. Di ples clean taim no dey. A glad fo dey fo hia.* (Singapore is very beautiful. The place is beautifully clean. I'm very happy to be here.) Look at the stringing out of their limited vocabulary! A book means a letter, or a report, anything written, and it has by the grace of God retained the original meaning, a book. Just because 150 or 200 million people speak assorted abortions of English, it doesn't mean that a new language has been created. (Maybe we have to define *language*.)

We ask you; can any woman respond to the Cameroon pidgin of *You're beautiful!* when it is some inchoate pidgin mumbling that she gets by the *pass mark*?

plain water   Toh Paik Choo (ref. 20) points out that like the French the Chinese never order water. But the reasons are different. It's nothing to do with the Chinese tea drinking that controlled waterborne disease and allowed them to swell their population to a billion with unbridled abandon. She says they need the two syllables to make them feel comfortable linguistically: *plain water*. They say *white rice* when ordering plain boiled rice. An interesting explanation.

ploblems   We don't seem to have too many problems in Singapore; just *ploblems*, *porblems*, and *prablems*; the last not quite like the American *prarblem*. *Pobblums* also pop up now and then. And a real favourite phrase is "No ploblem!"

pluck   Fruits are never ever picked off a tree here. They are always *plucked* off trees.

poe-ette   *Poets* are split into two distinct syllables. These split personalities write *poe-ems*. The latest NUS English graduates' version is *poh-yems*.

prayer Pronounced like *preyer* in Singlish and not *prar*, as in our dictionary. While we are on the subject of prayer, we'll quote a prayer written by one of our older Singaporean friends.

MONUMENTAL PRAYER

Before I lay me down to sleep,
I pray the Lord my soul to keep,
and as I knelt to pray before,
my last prayers are for Singapore.

We thank you O Lord for the men who sacrificed their lives,
for these men and for their wives.
We thank you Lord for the lines they drew,
and the risks they took,
to castle us with knight and rook.
We thank you O Lord.

For the balance they chose between freedom and chains,
for setting their sights on tomorrow's gains,
for keeping themselves clean to the core,
for the strength and will to build Singapore.
We thank you O Lord.

Over the years we set our spines of steel;
We gave our all, but now we feel,
We must take back the other half,
Give us time to sing and laugh,
We beseech thee O Lord.

Give us this day our daily bread,
through the Finance Ministry,
in spite of being so badly bled,
by Mindef's spending spree,
And forgive the trespasses of the NWC
and the URA's sins against property.

Lord, would your ear be deaf,
to a prayer for the death of the SDF?
And will there be honey for our tea,
if you bless the EDB?

Our Father who art in heaven,
cut our Ministries down to seven,
and keep our Perm Secs clean with courage.
Kill the slowly growing cankers,
so selfish and sinister,
and give them the guts to say "no"
to the mighty Minister.

De Profundis, I cry to thee O Lord,
but lest I slip and betray,
the blackest, vilest thoughts in me,
I will not even try to pray for the University.

And do not forget to make all females free,
whether or not they have a degree.

Saints of the Golden Chersonese, Pray for us,
Saints of the Straits, Pray for us,
Saints of Singapore, Pray for us,
HDB, shelter us,
SSO, play for us,
CPF, save us,
PUB, enlighten us.
May all the statutories and quangos lessen their stress
  on kudo's
and make our children happy in the next century.

God!
Never in the history of man,
has any nation been able to plan,
and social-engineer a people as we can.
Send us the prophets, God,
to define our dreams.

Glory be to God for dappled things,
like our spotted education story,
of a plod through snaffled swings.

Let's not confuse horse and cart,
Let's concentrate on when they start,
Let's not wreck our tiniest tots,
in kindies led by untrained clots.
Let our finest graduates mould,
the pliable, tender six-year-old.

And, please God, make it the rule,
every child to the nearest school.
Please God try to stop the streaming;
Don't spoil the milk-mass with the creaming.

Lord, put our children back in the sun,
Let them shout and laugh and learn with fun.

Send us teachers with pride in their hearts,
teach them to stand sure without shuffling,
for in them is the future,
the Power and Glory,
of the flowering of our land.

Please God will you help me,
do this for my country.
I want to build a work of art,
somewhere in the city's heart,
a structure of monumental size,
to hold in front of the nation's eyes,
that they may see,
continuously,
lest they forget.

An arch of white towering high,
bright in the sun against our sky,
formed to the Normal Distribution Curve,
so that its Gaussian shape will serve,
as a constant reminder that humanity,
is a mixture of Mass and Minority,
Mankind is not a homogenous lump,
the majority lives under the hump,
but the bad and the best,
the scums and the creams,
lie within the tail extremes,
This let us not forget.

And below the arch, in its shade,
a cascade,
a continuous flowing flood,
of water dyed deep red as blood.
Amen.

pressurised A word Singlish has given a new meaning and works to death. That's the ray of hope: *pressurise* will die with overwork.

privacy The *pry* bit is accentuated in Singlish, ruining privacy. A mispronunciation that clashes with meaning.

prizes If you listen in to the share market report, don't jump to the conclusion that the Singapore Stock Exchange only offers win-win-win opportunities, as the announcer may read out the "Share market prizes ..."

pro-noun-see-a-tion We came across a howler once when the teacher being interviewed for a job told us that he always stressed the correct *proNOUNciation*; saying it in the Singlish version that emphasises the two (yes, two) syllables in *noun*. And since we have quoted a teacher, we will quote from Crewe (ref. 5): "The situation then becomes self-perpetuating as the generation with reduced competence rise to be teachers and examples (writers, bosses, administrators, etc.) of the younger generations."

public relation Not everybody's uncle, but a plural slip.

punchet The Malay version of *punctured* is often used, but we are not always sure that the users know they are using a Malay word.

purchase The *chase* is enunciated clearly, wrongly, in Singlish. And the second syllable is always wrongly stressed. A very common error. It should be *per'chesing*.

put It is strange how Singlish takes an English verb and uses it where another should be used; and as if to maintain the balance of its odd errors, applies the other where the first should be used. Singlish gives *put* and *wear* this treatment. A common description: "I am thin and have buckteeth. I am hollow-cheeked, balding and I put on spectacles." See **wear** and compare.

The abuses of *put* do not stop here. There are umpteen variations. One is, "I am putting up at Queenstown," not that some unfortunate aunt is putting up with him.

Anthea Fraser Gupta (ref. 6, p. 33) makes an interesting statement on *put*: "Sentences such as 'She put the car in the garage' are widely rejected by undergraduates and schoolteachers because of a rule that the word 'put' can only be used with portable objects."

We have only one entry for Q. (Our Scrabble fanatic friend asked us to put in a plea that the Q piece be marked QU.)

quarterly "How often does it happen?"
"Three months once."
Singlish puts the key figure first.

R

RP Received Pronunciation, the linguistics people's term for that 'perfect' English way of talking once known as a BBC or an Oxford accent to some. Adam Brown points out in ref. 6 that "RP is spoken by very much a minority in Britain, 10 at a generous estimate ... and 3 to 5 percent as a perhaps more realistic figure ..." Mr Brown also states that "RP pronunciations from non-native (including EMS) speakers are often judged to be "affected" or "putting on airs".

> [Adam Brown] puts forward various criteria for establishing priorities for teachers in this part of the world; in particular the need to examine not only RP vowels but also the vowels of speakers in Singapore and Malaysia to see what the differences are and whether these differences are important with regard to hindering communication in the context of using English for international communication.
> —J.A. Foley (ref. 6, p. xviii)

rack-reck-rich-rock-ruck-rook-mate-mete-mite-more-mute-mare-mere-mire-move-mure-part-pert-port-oh-awl-boor-cow-dowry-chin-go-bang-so-ship-thin-the-rouge This is not Singlish gibberish.

Puzzle: What do these word have in common?

Answer: They are the key words used as references for pronunciation in the *Little Oxford English Dictionary*.

They are printed at the bottom of every page. The series spreads over the bottom lines of four pages. There is an important practical implication for Singaporeans who are looking up the dictionary to check pronunciations. If they cannot pronounce these correctly, they will never improve.

We will give one piece of advice to those who want to improve their pronunciation by quoting a Japanese proverb. "Ask once and you will be embarrassed once. Don't ask; you'll be embarrassed for life."

raid The colour, strong and striking; not a sudden incursion by the police embarrassing you.

read up "Where did you read that up?" Compensates for leaving out the *up* in pick up.

reefer It was a dimly lit, intimate type of bar. Slimy men hunched over their glasses; thin evil-eyed greasy types looking like drug pushers; women in the dark dressed with promises of earthy pleasure.

In the mood of the night the saxophone wailed out the old familiar melody and the singer purred into the microphone: "Moon Reefer ... wider than a mile ..."

reevit Once used in shipbuilding, but these days found most often on jeans.

regarding *Regarding about the meeting today ...* While Singlish hacks some things down to the core sounds, it is sometimes generous in grammar with its redundancies.

Another misuse of *regarding* is, *This is regarding what?* A favourite of secretaries.

relaxation exercises A cassette tape produced by the "Minstry of Helt" on relaxation exercises has some howlers. It has the usual *ders* and *clothings* and two new ones: *deeber*, for deeper, and letting the sun *bask on you*.

rented It was the first sentence in the *Straits Times* article headed, "Charge of the Light Brigade", on 20 July 1991: "The shrill shriek of a siren rented the air …" *Rent* (as *tear*) is also *rent* in the past tense. A letter of credit, meaning a landlord of good reputation, however, could have rented a flat to you, but not the air.

repute From an advertisement: "We are reputated to cater for all occasions with capacity of 120 tables and ample parking lot."

retrench This word is widely used in the sense of laying off staff. Its *Oxford Paperback Dictionary* meaning is to reduce the amount of (retrench one's operations) or to reduce one's expenditure or operations, for example *We shall have to retrench*. In Singlish the implication of retrenching is invariably reduction of staff.

rich A nice one uttered by an advertising type. She used the phrase *audience rich*. We thought it was very innovative, but it turned out to be audience reach.

right? This word in its interrogative tone gets to some Singaporeans like nicotine, alcohol and drugs. These *right?* addicts end every sentence of statement with "right?"

A growing body of children entering the formal school system will have a knowledge of English although it may be of a colloquial variety. This body of knowledge should not be regarded simply as an 'unacceptable' form of English but as a starting point for the development of a continuum of English from informal to formal which the child can use in the appropriate social setting. —J.A. Foley (ref. 6, p. xix)

roaster *The boss gave me the roaster* does not mean what you may think. *Roaster* in Singlish is roster in English.

roat Bukit Timah Roat.

Rose-Mary Always pronounced as two female names, Rose and Mary. In a way akin to the strawberry mispronunciation.

S

sales In *Made in Singapore*, the authors point out that sales people here tend to say "I am in the sales line." We have often come across this. The telephone interview we recently had with an applicant for a sales job is typical:

"What's your present job?"

"I'm in the sales line."

"What are you selling?"

"Consumer."

"What sort of consumer products are you selling?"

"Oh ... things for the house."

"What things? Vacuum cleaners?"

"Not essactly ..."

"What do you mean ... Are you selling vacuum cleaners, or not?"

"Well yes; but it is a very different kind of vacuum cleaner."

"Oh that new thing ... the Spectra?"

"Yes. That's it."

"What were you doing before that?"

"I was in technical."

"Technical?"

"Yeah, industrial centrifuge servicing."

"Why did you leave that job?"

"Because I had to travel too much. Besides I wanted to go into the sales line."

"Travel? Overseas?"

"No Johor only lah. I was overall in-charge of all of Johor."

"Oh … I see … How long have you been in sales?"

"Quite some times …"

sall-mon An example of a mute consonant not dropped. This one is a Singapore Standard. EVERYBODY says *sal-mon* with the *l* quite clear. No one has ever told them the *l* is mute.

scared Still heard in school playgrounds: "You tink I scared of you ha!" The word is sometimes pronounced *scat*.

scold Platt, Weber and Ho (ref. 15) state: "'Scold' is used in SgE (Singapore English) where many other varieties of English would now use expressions such as 'tell-off', 'tick-off'."

One still hears, "Doan scoal me now. I crashed the car."

scrapegoat Quite common. Scapegoat; skap; a goat on which the high priest laid the sins of the people and then sent away into the wilderness; one made to bear blame due to another.

search Singlish speakers often use the word *search* when *look for* should be used.

"What the Dickens is Grandpa doing out there in the dark?"

"He's searching for the plier he left there."

seegret Cigarette. Here's one for smokers. Sir Thomas Sopwith, the designer of the Sopwith Camel, said when he gave up smoking, "It's bad for me." He was 94 then.

seek Ill, indisposed. Pronounced to rhyme with Sikh. *Sick* and *ill* are often used with complete interchangeability in Singlish.

seen Either *sin* or the past tense of *to see*. And since we have mentioned sin, we'll list four of Kachru's 'Seven Attitudinal Sins' which English language teachers could be guilty of:
- The sin of not recognising the non-native varieties of English as culture-bound codes of communication.
- The sin of ignoring the systemicness of non-native varieties of English.
- The sin of ignoring linguistic interference and language dynamics.
- The sin of exhibiting language colonialism.

Are these sins to you?

Seenks, Sinks There's an Ah Beng one on this. Looking at a sign outside a kitchen fittings shop which read *Aluminium Sinks*, Ah Beng remarked, "I know dat!"

sees Not *cyst*, but *sister*. Short for *seester*.

seeve-out Sieve out. Few Singaporeans know that it is pronounced *siv*.

seksy Pronounced with a hard *k* in Singlish.

sell-feesh Not fishmongering, but selfish.

semen The *semen store* is not the sperm bank, but the cement store. We feel we should also draw the attention of new expatriates to the Malaysian spelling of cement, SEMEN. Heidi Munan in her *Culture Shock Borneo* also cautions the visitor that the Malay word for paint is *cat* (pronounced *chut*); and large cans labelled *cat semen* only contain cement paint.

send *I'll send you to the airport.* Air parcel post?

severn Not the river in England, but the number.

sewwtch Those silent men who excavate the holes in our roads, turn the valves, throw the switches and rush out in the dead of night when a pump fails, have always been exasperated by the layman's confusion of the base words of their profession. One of them, sensitive to the fine arts (yes, there are men with fine aesthetic feelings in the department) and to the English language in particular, once burst out in a fit of anger, "Shit! [They seldom use that four-letter word.] When will people learn! Sewerage is the whole system of sewers, pumps, valves, treatment works ... the lot. Sewage is the stuff the sewers carry. I'm sick to the back teeth of people ringing up and asking us to please come and fix their 'sewwtch'."

Did you know that there was another meaning to *sewer*? Pronounced the same way (su'er), it is an officer who arranged the dishes at a feast, placed the guests, etc. Shitty job.

Talking of sewerage reminds us of a friend who was building his own house and received a quotation for the septic tank which he thought was astronomically high. So he decided to read up on the subject and check the design out himself. He wasn't an engineer; he was a newspaper reporter. He left us and went to the National Library. We met him two days later and asked how his research on sewerage was progressing. "Oh," he replied, "I've forgotten that. The trouble was that the next word in the encyclopedia after 'sewerage' is 'sex'."

sex A review of Catherine Lim's short story collection, *Shadow of a Shadow of a Dream*, in the *Straits Times* of 20 August 1988, by Helen Chia, starts off with "No sex please, we're Singaporean". Almost British, but not really our colonial heritage. More like the new Asian social reticence still trying to model itself on Victorian morality. Or should we say Christian morality?

Generally Singaporeans handle this well; the pronunciation, the grammar, filling forms, the animal and social aspects.

> **The problem with a lot of material used for teaching English in the Singaporean school system is that it is EFL orientated, suitable perhaps in a country where little or no English is spoken outside the classroom.**
>
> —J.A. Foley (ref. 6, p. 57)

sexsual We have heard it; a softer sound of things connected with sex. Perhaps a hitherto undiscovered subtle melding of *sex* and *sensual*. In our dictionary, it's sek'su-al.

shao-wer Shower. The *were* component comes out strong. The purists of vocabulary would rather hear *shower* said badly than accept *bath* for *shower*. Our dictionary reads, *shou'er*.

sheeps Either more than one sheep ... or several ships. A flock or a fleet.

sheepyard We have no sheep in Singapore but have a thriving *sheep repairing* industry. And the NPB (National Productivity Board) is screaming *higher productivity* all the time. The message is getting through to the workers ... most of the time.

This Singlish conversation which we overheard shows that the message gets distorted at times.

"You are working at Bishun Sheepyard; isn't it?"

"Yah."

"How long you been working there?"

"Quite long. About six mun. But I'm tinking of leaving."

"Why?"

"I doan find the work so productive."

shifting Moving house is often described as *shifting*.

shillings The older people here still refer to coins as *shillings*. A colonial hangover.

shot *Short* is pronounced in Singlish, more logically, *shot*, instead of long in proper RP style. *Long* is correspondingly pronounced *lorng* with a little bit of a drawl to ensure that the meaning is conveyed by the sound. It should be a short sound in RP.

show Young people today use the word to mean a movie: *Let's go to a show*.

"How do you spend your weekend or leisure times?"

"I go for shows."

side Another redundant word shoved in:

I'm living Jurong side. (Originated from *West Side Story*?)

I'm on the slender side.

I am a graduate from the building side.

Children should not run out from the backsides of buses. (Tongue, ref. 21)

silens Conversation about the police:

A: "Should we do something about the disturbing increase of police silens?"

B: "You mean not giving us the facts?"

A: "No lah! The noise of the police silens, lah."

We have some thoughts on silence. Silence is for the mystics. Silence will stop a lot of dreadful Singlish but it will still exist with its distortions in the mind as music buzzed in the head of the deaf Beethoven. It must be spat out of the system. Whatever you do, do not follow the implied advice of that interesting book, *The Wisdom of the Desert* by Thomas Merton: "It was said of Abbot Agatho that for three years he carried a stone in his mouth until he learned to be silent."

silver service We thought we heard *silver service*, but it really was *siver* and he meant *civil* service.

simply *Simply* often occurs unexpectedly, for example *The organisation has crumbled to such a state that we simply can't go on.*

Salesgirl to browser in bookshop: "Can I help you?"

"No tanks, simply looking."

Sing-dollar This lovely abbreviation of the Singapore dollar was probably created when the first yelps of *yuppies* began to be heard across the land. It is music to them. It sings! Did you know the dollar sign came from the figure of eight which was stamped on the old Spanish pieces of eight? (Ref. 9)

Singapore The name of our country is actually an Anglicised version of the Indian word *Singapura*. We accept this with equanimity knowing that the English have permanently distorted the names of so many countries and cities all over the world; Nippon was turned into Japan, Roma to Rome, etc. In fact, Winston Churchill in his pompous way made the English attitude quite clear: "Everybody has a right to pronounce foreign names as he chooses."

But the fair name of Singapore has also been twisted to suit Mandarin and Hokkien. With the overwhelming majority of Chinese in our population, and the great national drive to promote Mandarin, should we not use *Sin-chia-po* (*Xin Jia Por* in Hanyu Pinyin), just as the Japanese know their own country as Nippon and ignore what the world calls them? At least most of our people will pronounce it right.

singer Overheard at a restaurant:
"Lily, can you play singer on Saturday?"
"No lah! I not that good."
"Come on; it's only our own company staff lah."
"No. Truly. I can't play singer."
"Don't be like that lah. You are good."
"No. I cannot. I'll play darbles. Last time my smash was so strong. But now lousy lah."

Singerlish This may be a better name for our variety of Ingerlish.

Singh It strikes us as an example of failure to appreciate each other's cultures in our tolerant and understanding society when we hear a Singaporean say "Mr Singh". We don't expect all Singaporeans to know about the intricacies of turbans and the significance of the Five Appurtenances of the Sikhs, but we do expect them to know that *Singh* is like the Japanese *San*, that our Israeli friends don't eat pork and the French are horrified at our drinking VSOP brandy with water. After all, every Singaporean knows the meaning of *bai*, brother, and they have dozens of pun-jokes on the word.

Singlish We are trying to collect samples of Singlish in this glossary. As one would expect, we found most of it at the lower levels of education. After searching at the lower limits of Singlish we turned around and looked at the upper limits of Singlish.

Who speaks and writes the Singlish? A few brought up in homes with a true English-speaking environment; products of a second generation of Singaporeans and Malaysians who had striven for language perfection, descendants of the Babas, children of parents with an overseas education or of mixed marriages, people who have lived overseas, etc. Fortunately, because their English is their strength, many of them find employment in positions that influence large numbers of Singaporeans. Where are these people? Where the business is the English language; teachers of English in the tertiary institutions and our schools, journalists, copywriters, scriptwriters, editors, publishers ... There is hope if these people maintain their English standard, but Singlish will take over if they set poor examples.

There are also Singaporeans in regular close contact with English speakers, business and technical people, who maintain a standard close to the Singlish-English divide. We haven't had the skills nor the time to look at the people at the boundary layers. We know we should if we are to examine Singlish closely and stratify it into levels. It is only such quantitative and selective scrutiny that will bring us a step further in sorting out the grain from the chaff of Singlish.

One more thought. Does this plugging of good English not create a new class barrier? Or has it already done so?

"… there are some 20 percent of the younger generation of Chinese who are not comfortable in the English language," said Lee Kuan Yew (*Straits Times*, 18 May 1992). We think Mr Lee has underestimated the percentage.

Whatever it is, Singlish has its charm and its funny face. We tried to capture some of this with our distortion of the old film song:

THE SOUNDS OF SINGLISH

My ears are alive to the sounds of Singlish,
It twists in my guts like a thousand spears,
My senses are dulled and I can't distinguish,
the true from the false,
in the sounds of Singlish,
and I weep in pain, my eyes full of tears.

My heart wants to throb to the beat of the bards
that sang of the lakes and the trees,
My heart wants to sigh with a rhyme that flies
from the lips like a breeze,
to laugh like a snob as I listen to Singlish all day,
to sing through the night as I stagger down Ang Moh
   Kio Way.

I go to the stalls when my heart is lonely,
I know I will hear what I've heard before,
My heart will be wrung with the sound of Singlish,
And I'll cry once more …

sir An example of the very common Singlish twist of *sir* is "Our school is one of the few girls-only schools in Singapore, but we have two sirs." *Sir* is a male teacher.

sit We do not know how to classify this one. One is often asked by the receptionist to "have a sit". Does she err in pronouncing *seat*, or is she offering you the hospitality of a *sit*, as in the invitation "Have a drink"?

skew me Excuse her; it's the education system.

skimped *I skimped quickly through the book.* Meaning: I skimmed through the book.

skive This verb, which is used in some parts of the United Kingdom but is not found in many English dictionaries, has appeared out of the blue in Singapore. It is used by NSmen and means to cheat, to hide, to run away from one's duty. We find it strange. Perhaps some colonial British military unit seeded the thing.

skrap Commonly mispronounced part of the phrase *skrap and grovel*.

sky-juice A lovely euphemism for water. No one would bat an eyelid if you ordered *sky-juice* at a food centre. Jus' water.

sleeper Footwear; not the railway words for a bed or a piece of timber on which the rails are bedded.

slipping *He's slipping on the job.* May mean that he's slipping, or that he's sleeping. It doesn't matter anyway. If the fellow's 'slipping', sack him.

slow by slow We mourn the passing of this lovely laid-back gem of earlier Singlish. The old sign, *Slow Men at Work*, has also gone. Does the disappearance of so many Singlish terms mean there is an improvement in Singapore English? We think it definitely does not. Singlish expressions are changing, making it difficult to keep in step with the Tans.

We have read (ref. 5) that there was once a great vowel shift in Britain; when the pronunciation of *house* changed from rhyming with *goose* to its present status, and *goose* changed from rhyming with *close* (a close thing) to rhyming with *moose*, etc. But that was in the beginning of the 15th century. We think Singlish pronunciations, word usage and grammar are changing faster than its parent. Happens all the time …

social significance With all the politicians who exhort Singaporeans to be perfect citizens, and some crazy suggestions that novelists should write about political and social themes rather than love, horror and mystery, perhaps this old song from the musical *Pins and Needles* (words and music by Harold Rome) should be blared out by RCS every morning:

> Sing me a song of social significance
> all other tunes are taboo.
> I want a ditty with heat in it
> appealing with feeling and meat in it.
> Sing me a song of social significance
> or you can sing till you're blue.
> Let meaning shine from every line
> or I won't love you.

soh The *o* diphthong in its Singlish way. There is also an occasional grammar misuse of *so* as in *I doan tink so I can do dat*.

sole-der Solder. No one seems to get this right. It should be sol-der, the first syllable rhyming with *all*, *ball*, *call*. We heard one variation on this; shouldering iron.

sooger Sugar with the first syllable rhyming with *sue*, and a stress on the *ger*. Very, very common, our special Singapore sugar. Our dictionary reads, *shu'ger*; perhaps it should be written, *shuger*.

soot At the height of a soccer match you will hear *Soot!* shouted with great excitement. It is *not* a Singlish twist of *shoot*. It is a Cantonese word meaning to shoot, to attack.

sort Short. Not very common: *I have sort hair.*

specialist Many examples of the verb *to specialise* are being used incorrectly in advertisements: *We are specialist in ...*

speet "He was speeting and the policeman caught him."
"How terribly embarrassing!"
"Yes, he was speeting so fast."
"He's a fast spitter?"
"Yah ... prrrrr like dat ... over hundret kilometre."

spend me Treat me to something. This is certainly not English. The American writer Tom Wolfe would agree with us wholeheartedly. He once wrote, "There are certain restaurants in New York where if an upper-class Englishman picks up the bill the whole table rises up and applauds."

spick Speak. Does sloppy speaking reflect a sloppy mind? We also once heard, "Speak it a little louder." It prods us to quote twice from Ludwig Wittgenstein, "Everything that can be said can be said clearly." "Whereof one cannot speak, thereof one must be silent."

spoilt *Sorry lah, we have no ice ... the fridge is spoilt.* Not the food in the fridge; the fridge sometimes gets spoilt, like motors, switches, taps, etc.

SQ Singaporeans have adopted this prefix for Singapore Airline flights to refer to the airline. It is a strange adoption. There is a special SIA Singlish (or should we say *SQ* English?), a high flying sub-variety. Three samples from *Sunday Times* (7 May 1989) are:
- Startled passengers on a Singapore Airlines flight could hardly believe their ears when a stewardess announced: "We will now be serving snakes."
- "Ladies and gentlemen, some of our cabin crew will be rolling down the aisles in a few minutes. They will be selling spiritual items, cigarettes and perfumes."
- And then there was the case of the Singapore Girl who left a cabin full of red faces in her wake. It was time for light refreshments and they were serving Swedish meatballs in first class. Her innocent query: "Sir, would you like sauce on your balls?"

sting *That dirty toilet ... it really sting!* We know what he means. Ammonia has that effect.

der toilet sting

stinge *Although he was drawing a good salary he stinged on food.* (He most probably was not Chinese.) An original Singlish creation.

stint This word seems to be used by civil servants quite accurately, although they may not realise it. They keep referring to their stint in such-and-such a department, unaware that a stint implies one only does the allocated amount of work. It carries an implication of being an unpleasant task.

stood-dent A Singapore-bred twist of *student*, the first syllable neither rhyming with the English *stew* nor with the American *stuu* (both delicious dishes), but with a stress on a clipped *stood*. The Singlish pronunciation of *student* is indeed a true native creation.

straw-bay-ree The fruit. Same for *ras-bay-ree*, *gooze-bay-ree*. *Berry* as *bayree* seems to be quite difficult to correct. Perhaps they should teach schoolchildren the old *Boy's Own Paper* bit about the customer who complained to his grocer, Mr Berry, and make them say it till they get it right: "Here's a pretty mull, Berry. You sent me a bill, Berry, before it was due, Berry. Your father the elder Berry wouldn't have made such a blue, Berry! I'm not a goose, Berry, and you needn't look so black, Berry, because I don't care a straw, Berry, and shan't pay you till the winter, Berry."

stun As in *go-stun*, it means reverse, go astern. A backward directive, not a positive one like "Go stun her with your charm!"

stylo Swanky, stylish. A poetic variation is *stylo-mylo*.

sue The Singaporean would say, "Sister Soosee suing sirts for sojers," mispronouncing *sew*.

suntan *Usually I go to the beach for sun tanning. When I'm free I go for those sun tanning.* Both quotes from SBC interviews with the public.

suppose "But, mama, the low neckline is suppose to catch the eye!"
"You'll catch a cole!"
"Yah, but I'll catch my man!"

sworllen Spelling this out was difficult. The first part is like *swirl* with an *o* sound; almost like *squall*. It is a full sound; puffy, mouthed with a rounded *whore* sound mixed with overtones of *opulence* and *swallow*. The Singlish *swollen* is a unique sound.

syllable This was indeed a howler! A Singapore woman who spoke English very well was criticising Singlish pronunciation: "One of the most common faults is putting the accent on the wrong syl-labb-ble," she said, putting her accent on the *second* syllable. Adam Brown, in ref. 6, states that EMS speakers, whose rhythm is typically not stress-based, make little differentiation between stressed and unstressed syllables.

On another note, we heard an amusing one when we asked a graduate how she prepared herself to teach a subject she had not even studied at 'A' level. "First ting, I look at the syllable."

T

t Fowler dwells at some length on the silent *t* in English. *T* is mute in *castle*, *listen*, *fasten*, *bustle*, etc. He notes that the *t* in *pestle* is being sounded; so is the *t* in *often* in some circles, and he takes heart in the continuing silence of the *t* in *softens*.

taber Table. The same erring occurs in *pickle*.

take As in *Do you take durians?* Chinese and Malay do not substitute the verb *to eat* with a similar verb *to take*. French does in some cases, with *prend*. Another example: *I have just taken my dinner.*

Is *I am taking Economics* Singlish?

I take a bath every morning is perhaps correct English but the common British usage would be *I have a bath every morning*.

take cover An NS phrase for *skive*.

tan cheak peng A soldier with no money, NS slang.

tearter As in the *Kallang Tearter*. Tongue (ref. 21) points out that the English only use *theatre* for live theatre and not for the cinema as Singaporeans and Americans do.

teats Listen carefully to the context if *teats* is said loudly and boldly in public. Even if *milk teats* are mentioned, it could be the pronunciation and grammatical error of *teeths*.

What is Singlish? Define it. See *Singlish*.

teen *Thin* or *tin* or *teen*.

telling A verb form Indians are prone to slip into. Instead of *He said*, they use *He was telling*.

TESL All Singapore teachers know these initials for teaching English as a Second Language, and many of them have been to such courses which vary widely in quality. Mr C.H. Practor took a mighty swipe at TESL a few years ago (ref. 11), but it's not what he said about TESL that we want to raise. We quote from his paper a fundamental point that is at variance with what many linguistics pundits in Singapore believe. "… the heretical tenet … that is best, in a country where English is not spoken natively but is widely used as medium of instruction, to set up the local variety of English as the ultimate model to be imitated by those learning the language." Will you ponder on this?

thent Very, very common. A standard threat phrase in Singlish is *Thent you know!* or *Thent you see what happen!* "If you doan do your homework and fail the exam you'll have to sweep the streets. Thent you know!" The way some Singaporeans say *then* with a *t* ending has puzzled us for years. We are not sure, but we think those who went through the Chinese education stream in the old days are more prone to say *thent*. But we cannot see how the Chinese language sounds cause this. The younger set say *den* instead of *thent* or *then*.

thia boh NS slang for *to hear nothing, understand nothing*.

this *You can take this number 171 bus to Bukit Timah.* Quite a new thing with JC (junior college) folk. They do not say, "There is a girl I have a crush on" but start sentences in the form, "There is this girl … or boy, or book …" Or if they start an anecdote about a soldier, it begins with, "There was this soldier …" We can't figure out how this has happened.

those *Those job with a well defined duties and responsibilities …*

This is what the bright young man, whose only job interview apparent flaw was the English of his Singlish education, wanted: clear duties, clear responsibilities; everything in a crystal morning-sun long-shadow clarity. He couldn't face the *unks* (space scientists' jargon for *unknowns*). How is he going to tackle the *unk-unks*; the *unknown unknowns*?

tidak-apa *No big deal* in Malay.

Perhaps the *tidak-apa* attitude was best summarised in the philosophy of a frien' of ours, "Narting big deal lah!"

We love this hang-loose approach to life but our enthusiasm is dampened by Mick Jagger's advice, "It's all right letting yourself go, as long as you can let yourself back." A lot of those creative songwriters are equally creative in language.

ti-ert Josephine: "Not tonight lah! I so ti-ert." Our NS men get really *ti-ert* at times and have to force themselves to think happy thoughts when they are near the end of their tether. It only works initially and when the real *shag* feeling comes down on them, all the happy thoughts fade. Even 'tinking of your arlohdee' doesn't work.

Takut bin Salah tried to capture this in a rap. But we have to top up your vocabulary before you can understand it:

Charbor = girl, woman (Hokkien)

Lagi satu = one more (Malay)

Untuk = for, in the sense of for Singapore (Malay)

Pua-see = half dead (Hokkien)

GSO = General Staff Officer, which is described in *Army Daze* as "also Girls Supply Officer at army parties"

Idle king = the epitome of idleness; NS slang

Bozo = clown, fool; NS slang

Sabo = sabotage, ruin. NS slang

Sudah = have become (Malay)

Lembeh = limp, soft, weak (Malay)

Toe-jam = either Singapore foot or the dirt between one's toes, or sticky, mucky stuff one finds in canvas shoes (old Singlish, revived in NS slang)

Kuda = horse (Malay)

PTI = Physical Training Instructor

Chern hai = really, truly (Cantonese)

Beh tahan = fagged out, cannot take it any more (Hokkien)

Chiak her = literally to eat fish; a strict officer (Hokkien)

LAP RAP

Go for der next one, der Singapore lap,
Bang on der drum lah, let my feet tap, tap,
Gimme fierce music, cos I wanna rap,
Sing as your feet move, let your hans clap, clap.

Imagine yourr dere, on der disco floor,
Dancing like for real, with a live charbor,
Body all paining, like never before,
Lagi satu lap, untuk Singapore.

For der udder lap, we mus' go, go, go,
Not like pua-see girls, from the GSO,
Keel der idle king, who is slow, slow, slow,
Doan let dat bozo, dis one lap sabo.

Got anarder one, lap for Singapore,
Maybe after dat, anarder one more,
Legs sudah lembeh, an' feet getting sore,
Shoes full of toe-jam, blisters now all raw.

Running round der square, like kuda, clop, clop,
PTI yelling, darble up! chop! chop!
Chern hai, beh tahan. Man, I wanna drop,
When will the chiak her tell us we can stop.

times "How long have you been with Wing, Kong and Sons?"

"Quite some times."

"I didn't do this during working hours. I took my personal times to do it." Rather rare.

"I couldn't lah. The time was quite clash with …" Also not very common.

"It can save a lot of times if you use …"

"At that times I was very, very fat."

tingle We came across this mix-up of two words once and our first reaction was shock at the brazenness of the young girl who shouted out to her boyfriend, "Give me a tingle tomorrow." Tinkle, of course.

tinkle Sometimes confused with *tinker* as in, "Don't tinkle with it lah!"

A correction of a staff report tickled us. The typed report stated, "… he is very interested in computer and has a PC at home which he tickles with." A ballpoint scrawl had scratched the error and written over it, *tinkles*.

tiok beh pio To strike a lottery in Hokkien, but in NS slang it means to find your name on the roster for guard duties.

tok Talk. The people from Papua New Guinea pronounce it the same way. They also have an expression, *one tok*, meaning speaking the same language.
In Singlish we are united in *one tok*. But is it really 'One Tok'?

tomattoe Tomato pronounced neither with the true RP *toe-mah-toe* nor with the American *toe-may-toe*, but with a Singaporean innovation neither here nor there; in *to-mat-to*, the middle syllable rhymes with *rat*.

This falling in between is similar to the Singlish for *student*. They are native creations. Maybe we should go back to the old description of tomatoes; love apples (ref. 9).

topo king One who is bad at map reading and gets lost; NS origin.

trace back One of the Singlish redundancies akin to *buy back* but quite different to *hark back*. We saw this in a book published in Singapore. It raises the question that if Singapore editors cannot see the subtler forms of Singlish in manuscripts, our published material will add to the bad influences on young Singaporean minds struggling with the complexities of the English language.

SBC was often a bad influence. Radio Heart oozes Singlish *allatime*, but it makes no pretence of being a model of English. Radio Heart zooms into the hearts of Singaporeans and does not let fringe considerations distract it from its target – Chinese dialects and Singlish slop around all day. But Radio Heart did once have an interesting slot for 'The Grammar Man'.

Our monopoly newspaper is full of Singlish, probably because the subeditors do not see the subtler forms of it.

Don't we need an Ombudsman of English or a Watchdog Committee? But committees design camels…

trainings A typical question from a job applicant these days is, "What trainings does your company provides?"

A sign of the times; job applicants sit across the table negotiating, redeeming the original meaning of *interview*. Job applicants also do not turn up for interview appointments without a word or phone call of explanation. They are hitting back against the many Singapore companies who don't even send rejection postcards.

tree A simplification of the mouthing of *three* which once allowed Singaporeans full enjoyment of their joke that Tarzan's car is the Mazda *tree-to-tree*.

turd *This is a turd class dump* only means that it rates as a third-class place in the speaker's opinion, without any crude derogatory emphasis.

turn out Sometimes one hears the Singlish version of how things *turn out*: "About your applications to study oversea. How was the turn out?"

turtel Turtle turned *turtel* in Singlish.

twelerff The number between *elayven* and *tirteen*.

two times *I've been there two times.* The Standard English version would be *I've been there twice.* Next in frequency is, of course, *tree times*.

U

Is Singlish something unique? See *unik*.

udder Usually recognisable in the context of *der udder one*. There is also the related *udderwise*, which is *not* bovine mammary expertise.

unersty A telescoping of *university*.

unik *Very unique* is heard quite often, as if to be merely unique was not good enough.

One of our acquaintances once said that Singlish can be *very unik* if it continued to develop along three lines. It has been moving along these lines for years but these *unik* strains have been hidden by substandard grammar and pronunciations to suit Chinese and Malay ears (not their tongues?).

These three directions are:
- the immediate communication of a message without the unnecessary verbal dressing that the English delight in;
- the economy of breath; and
- the creation of expressions to fill in the voids that still stand empty, waiting for word artists to fill them and add an extra touch of richness to the English language.

What he meant is exchanges like this:

"How often does he come here?"

"Everyday, he comes here."

The key word is uttered first.

Immediate communication, he said, was getting the key words in right in front of the sentence. To hell with word order; time is money. (Anyway the English have got their word order all wrong as far as nouns and adjectives are concerned.)

Economy of breath is already being practised in slang all over the world. The wide use of abbreviations in Singlish is an example. Other examples are *high blerd* for high blood pressure, *frus* for frustrated, *sabo* for sabotage.

Creation of new words or phrases has started but still has a long way to go. *Buy-back*, and the use of *ever* to compliment *never* are examples of success but we still have to find the Singlish *bon apetit*.

unnerstan As in "Unnerstan?" The answer is usually *no*; as E.B. White said, "When you say something, make sure you have said it. The chances of your having said it are only fair." A complementary Singlish word is *unnerwear*.

up As often as *up* is dropped in *pick up*, the little preposition is added on unnecessarily in Singlish:

Write up the report.
Get the car aircon fixed up.
I always do some exercise in the morning before washing and dressing up. (Tongue, ref. 21)
I was called up for interview. (Article omitted.)
I can't cope up with my workload.
I'll ring him up today.

usage The Singlish accent is on *sage*.

use Often applied in Singlish where *wear* should be used: *I have never used spectacles.* Although it drifts all over the place this book is about the sounds and uses of words. We think they are important. But Ivy Compton-Bennet takes an extreme view: "We must use words as they are used or stand aside from life." (Ref. 4)

V

Valentine's day As in many other parts of the world, Singaporeans have dropped the prefix of the old St Valentine's day. In the seventies, a Valentine in American criminal jargon meant a one-year sentence. We don't know why. If we have messed it up one way in Singapore, the Japanese have really made a mockery of the delightful western practice of St Valentine's day cards; the senders sign them clearly. And some think the Japanese are inscrutable!

vehicle Educators should not push this one. It just can't be handled by our local vocal systems. Think of *veer* to get it right; *veer-kle*.

very Sometimes used incorrectly for emphasis: *very vital ... very essential ... very suitable for promotion.* This is another of those redundancies with which Singlish abounds. But even native speakers and writers of English keep adding the unnecessary extra words: enclosed within, end result, military bomber, congregate around, past history, close proximity, original source, proceed ahead, totally annihilate, daily journal, stupid idiot. L.M. Boyd (ref. 2) tells a story that brings out the moral of redundancies in language.

"Where I apprenticed in this dandy trade, the best of the newsmen wrote the tightest crispest copy. One turned in a story containing a sentence, 'Raise it up a little higher.' The city editor said, 'Son, here's why I'm your boss.' He struck out the word 'higher'. The managing editor, looking over his shoulder, said to him, 'Mister, here's why I'm *your* boss.' He struck out the words, 'up a little'."

vulch A JC term at one time. A vulch is a guy who specialises on picking up girls the other guys drop; from *vulture*.

W

wake up your idea A National Service scolding term for the 'blur'.

wallop There are two Singlish uses of *wallop*:
I'll wallop you if you do dat again!
The prawns were really good. Man, did we wallop!
Whack is sometimes substituted for wallop.

want *Want some pickle or not?* Singlish loves the statement followed by a question phrase.

war *A succession of wars* in Singlish may be another of those collective nouns like *a plate of crumpets, a pair of shrews, an anthology of pros* and *a blast of strumpets*. The Singlish speaker does not know that the *w* is mute in *whores*.

And while we have mentioned nouns of groups of sinful people, we add others for animals, and inanimate things which we have come across in *An Exaltation of Larks*, James Lipton, Penguin, the Ontario Council of Teachers of English publications, *Directions* and *Indirections*, and other publications:

A murmuration of starlings

A leap of leopards

A wince of dentists

A lurch of busses
A flush of plumbers
An acne of adolescents
A mass of priests
An unction of undertakers
A cell of biologists
A duel of swordfish
A repugnance of cockroaches
A pinch of crabs
A dash of greyhounds
A union of carpenter ants
A battery of electric eels
A pride of egoists
A fleet of frigatebirds
A bosom of titmice
A stretch of mussels
A lot of real estate agents
A dose of pharmacists

Word games such as these stimulate interest in the language and provide opportunities to learn new words.

ways *Being new, I'm still finding my ways around the department.* Another variation: *We've got to look at this from both way.*

wear *Wear your shoes!* The same command is applied to shirts, dresses and 'trouser'.

And when *wear* should be used, *put on* is sometimes applied incorrectly. We give an example of the correct grammatical use but incorrect pronunciation of *wear*. It also illustrates the problems other people have with

English. This conversation between Edward Lear and the German Pessimist is taken from *Edward Lear* by Angus Davidson, a Penguin book:

G.P.: You vear spectacles alvays?

E.L.: Yes.

G.P.: They vill all grack in India; vun pair no use.

E.L.: But I have many pairs.

G.P.: How many?

E.L.: Twenty of thirty.

G.P.: No good. They vill all grack. You should have got of silver.

E.L.: But I have several of silver.

G.P.: Dat is no use. They vill rust; you might got gold.

E.L.: But I have some of gold.

G.P.: Dat is more verse; gold is alvays stealing."

Wedd-nes-day In Singlish the stress is incorrectly on the *wed* bit. Here is a case where the Singlish speaker can go to town zedding away and she or he misses it. Our 'dick' says, *wenz'da*, or *wenz'di*.

weedow Not only a grass widow among the weeds; all widows. We wonder how many of you appreciate the complexity of the statement by the elder Mr Weller in the *Pickwick Papers*: "... more vidders is married than single wimin."

week "Once in a week ...," says Singlish.

weeseekey As in Hainanese-Singlish *weeseekey sohtar*. It's really quite sacrilegious the way *whisky* is mispronounced. Another Singlish one on whisky is *or-toh-tui*, which is from the Hainanese and means Black Label. It may interest our readers that the word *whisky* comes from the Irish, not the Scottish *usquefaugh*, meaning 'water of life'.

wha'for *Wha'for you wan' to buy this?* The *t* is not heard. It is replaced by what the linguistics people call a 'glottal stop'. Glottal is the adjectival form of glottis, which is the narrow aperture at the mouth of the windpipe in one's chest. Dilation and contraction of the glottis helps the modulation of one's voice. A *glottal stop* is thus a sudden cutoff of sound. Glottal stops in pronunciation leave the end of words unvoiced: froc' (frog), bum' (bump), por' (pork).

We quote R.K. Tongue (ref. 21): "A glottal stop, indicated here by the symbol /?/ occurs in many non-RP dialects in Britain. It is the sound which is heard in the middle of the word 'butter' when pronounced by a speaker of the Cockney dialect of London – 'bu/?/er'. It is interesting to note that British visitors sometimes describe ESM (English of Singapore and Malaysia) as resembling Cockney; when they do, it is this feature that has created this impression."

what *What* used in passing the buck:
"Why did you do this?"
"They say what!" (In other words, "They told me to do it." *What* is dragged for emphasis.)

what about yourself? A very popular conversation response phrase:
"How ole are you?"
"Twenty. What about yourself?" (Sometimes, "How about yourself?")

where Godfrey Harrison and Lim So Lin, in their article in *New Englishes* (ref. 6), point out that *where* in Chinese is often at the end of the sentence whereas English starts a question with *where*. They illustrate this with *Ta zai nali?* (He/she where?)

This brings to mind an anecdote which underlines the importance of the idiomatic aspects of languages. An Englishman who had learnt Mandarin went to China. He was entertained to dinner by a VIP and his wife, who was quite an attractive woman. In his western style he told her she was very beautiful. To his confusion, she replied, "Nali! nali!" Literally it was *where*; but it is used in Mandarin in such situations in the sense of "Where the blazes did you get such an idea!"

where got? Used in the sense of *That's impossible!* "Where got meaning?" is a real favourite.

Where you from? Another routine question that telephone girls put to you. Be prepared for it. Don't say "I'm from Singapore." Give the name of a company. If the name of your company is beyond the normal limits of the Singlish span, use the word *Atlas*. It's easy to say and neutral enough for you to add on a product or service name: Atlas Shoes or Atlas Toilet Cleaning Services or Atlas Superior Meats. It gives a nice big global impression. You can introduce yourself truthfully and properly after she has connected you. The important thing to understand is that you haven't a hope in hell of getting through if you can't give a company name in response to "Where you from?"

who The *who* errors that occur all over the world also appear in Singlish. Perhaps we can stop one of them by quoting the dialogue from a *Born Loser* strip:

A: So I've come to the profound conclusion … it's not what you know but who you know."

B: It's not who you know, it's *whom* you know.

There is no confusion between *who* and *where*. The fresh female 'grad' meant just what she said, "Four years in the University and look who it has got me?"

who said! A common phrase used to react to bits of scandal, surprising news, etc. concerning oneself. For example,

"Lohsie ahh … I hear you got new boyflen."

"Who said!"

Why? *Why can't the English teach their children how to speak?* Do you remember this song from the film *My Fair Lady*? We thought it could be adapted for Singapore.

> We wallow as urchins in a gutter,
> Marked by every syllable we utter,
> We should be hanging down our heads in shame,
> For the mangling of a language, we stand to blame,
>
> The language that they left us has gone cold,
> Now we walk Marina Square,
> Slurring Singlish everywhere,
> Throwing out a heritage we hold.
>
> Why must this Singlish be the tongue our children speak?
> This distorted language,
> This linguistic freak.
> The sounds of our ancestors intruding into our speech,
> Thrusting English accents out beyond our reach.
>
> You, boy, did you go to school?
> Why? You tink I is a fool?

No one taught him *think* instead of *tink*,
Listen to the *dats* and *dese*,
Hear the zeds in *chaze* the *geeze*,
And the ghastly *sting* in place of *stink*.

We push our children making such a fuss;
Science, CL2 and calculus,
While Singlish slowly isolates us.

Why can't we start to teach our children how to speak,
English in the proper way,
Of Britain or the USA,
And not Singlish watered down and weak.

A Singaporean's way of speech absolutely classifies him,
The Singlish that he talks,
Makes many people in the world despise him,
In spite of how he strives for all round *axcellence*.

Oh! When will we realise our Singlish is a freak?
Causing strain and aural pain to other people's ears,
And driving them to anguish close to tears.
We even have moments when English completely disappears.

Why can't we start to teach our children how to speak?
Chinese learn their Chinese,
The Greeks are taught their Greek.
In Indonesia every one is taught his Bahasa,
Malaysians learn Jawi with the blinding speed of lightning,
The Thais do theirs backwards, which is absolutely frightening,
But we in Singapore,
With our silly Singlish streak,
Why is our English,
Why must our English,
Be so weak?

why not? *Why you not want to come with us?* This is a form of the *Why not?* question with the *you* shoved in between.

We heard an interesting slant on this over the air recently. "In the UK," the speaker said, "If you put forward an unconventional proposal you will invariably be asked 'why?' But in Italy, they will say 'Why not?'" A case where the use of the apparently negative *not* reveals a more positive attitude.

why you don't *Why you don't complain to the boss?* Singlish for *Why don't you ...?*

why you worry! Though it is not Standard English, the meaning is clear. But one should note that its more common usage is not in the sense of *Why wally wally until wally wallies you*, but in the MYOB (mind your own business!) sense. MYOB was used a lot by schoolgirls once. It is strange that the first coin minted in America, in 1787, had the words 'mind your own business' on it.

wite White. But if you look up the dictionary to see what the right pronunciation is, you will meet, *hwit*. Does that help?

with *With*, like many other prepositions, gets its share of omissions in Singlish :
The police issued him a summons. (Tongue, ref. 21)
Please supply me a list of your requirements.
We must be provided the tools for the jobs.

wok If she tells you she's going for a *wok*, don't dream of new and exotic taste experiences. She's merely going to take some ambulatory exercise; or trying to get away from you. (Feminist readers should read *he* for *she*.)

womit Some Indians just cannot handle the *v*. One should be on the lookout for *wipers in the grass*, *prose and werse*, *Wolgar boatmen* and *marriage wows*. We think *marriage wows* is something else …

won A verb form of Singlish that is dying out is, "I won him at badminton." It would of course be correct if he was the object of her sporty wooing, but Singapore girls are not like that.

work towards Civil servants in Singapore do not apparently work *under* anyone; nor do they *report to* anyone. They work *towards* their superiors. It is a strange euphemism in the proud traditions of Civil Service – indirect statements that ensure no loss of oriental face.

would Crewe (ref. 5) points out that *would* presents problems in English to students all over the world, but says that errors of the usage of *would* are 'rampant' in Singapore.

We present some examples:

I hope this would meet with your approval.

I expected that you and your missus would be able to attend.

We hope that our Marti (MRT) would help to ease the city traffic. (MRT is Mass Rapid Transit. *Mati* is *death* in Malay.)

But the average Singaporean does not have to cope with the other *woods*. One timber inspector, after years of familiarity with different types of wood, wrote:

"Do you think that if I SPRUCE myself up and TEAK her out ROSEWOOD let me RUBBER CHESTNUTS and CEDAR? Or WOOD that JARRAH? WOOD she BOX me? Or should I CYPRESS myself, and PINE FIR the BEECH? I ASH you? What WOOD YEW do?"

write-off *Although he's so abrasive we should not write-off him.* Yeah, it's ticklish.

wurz *Worse* in Singlish. But in this case the *z* is not strong. A sound that is a sort of cross between *z* and *s* is used. Should we call this *half-zedding the s*?

SINGLISH CROSSWORD 1

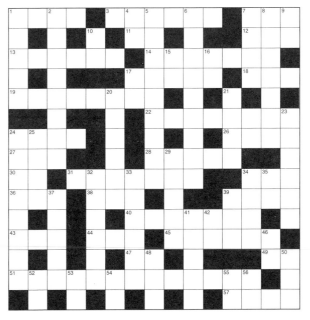

Cryptic Clues

Across
1. Feeling cold in Singapore with a merry old soul? (4)

3. Singlish for really good and not hollow. (6)
7. Copycat mammal? (3)
11. Refusal usually followed by a *lah* in Singlish? (2)
12. The river that is responsible for the mechanical Singlish sound of the city? (3)
13. AH! A gun! A mix-up! Whodunnit? Who did it? (6)
14. Of no importance in Singlish? (7)
17. Go and oil the house with a very light toilet. (5)
18. If Singlish created a new sound? (3)
19. A learner hissing strangely in a new variety of English? (8)
22. He works the controls in spite of the pea getting into the rotor. (8)
24. The cause of trouble can be a neverending misery in one's life. (4)
26. Giving something to the taxman every month? (4)
27. Covering it with a bit of a shrug? (3)
28. Thanks, Sue, for the quick fried potatoes. (5)
30. Pure chemicals in the bar? (2)
31. Keepers by common law? (7)
34. Is it almost a secure military organisation? (3)
36. That common Singlish error? (3)
38. One to a skylark from Shelley. (3)
39. Limping but not quite female. (4)
40. He was closest to him when Earnest cracked up. (7)
43. Without the head he's no intellectual. (3)
44. First back, small and charged. (3)
45. Singlish exhortation to dig deeper? (4,2)
47. First Italian person to handle data in and out of computers? (2)
49. Backward African country? (2)
51. Cleaner driving vehicle testers upset with one crying. (6,7)
57. Domestic Singlish? (4)

Down

1. Scrap of Singlish seafood. (5)
2. A little student making some money is a dangerous thing. (8)
4. A Singlish dialect switching verb. (2)
5. Yearning for a dwelling in the wilds? (4,5)
6. Full of mistakes ere our son unscrambled it. (9)
7. Pimples from a twisted cane? (4)
8. One who sits beside the concert pianist or looks after the end of the train? (4,3)
9. Take me as one sixth of an inch. (2)
10. Surprising Chinese surname? (2)
15. Albert is almost a friend without the softness. (2)
16. Towards the front of the tongue. (2)
20. An unchangeable physical characteristic of Singapore; it's not the sea. (6)
21. A grain without the seed is a criminal thing. (4)
23. He takes in some sail on a Singlish river. (6)
24. Singlish family members who we hear want to be Singlish steerers? (8)
25. Not quite an aural air but an atmosphere. (4)
29. Singlish sound of English exclamation? (5)
32. One of the elements of the sea? (6)
33. A menace of a lad who did an immoral act backwards. (6)
34. A Japanese surname of a man going to South Africa. (4)
35. Mother somersaulted in the morning. (2)
37. In a medicinal anti-germ concoction put on the buttocks by Singaporeans. (5)
39. Well-known school of Southeast London? (3)
41. He pores confused over the rules to learn these quickly. (5)
42. Spanish equivalent of the backward French. (2)
46. A Singlish expression used when giving up an article not usually available or applicable? (2)

48. Sounds surprising to be beholden to. (3).
50. One is often asked to have this in Singlish while waiting. (3)
52. Box for leisure. (2)
53. A hesitant Chinese surname? (2)
54. Heads of the thoracic and bronchial units deal with this disease once a major killer in Singapore. (2)
55. Measure yourself backwards. (2)
56. A school for creative monarchs in London? (2)

Simple Clues

Across

1. Cold in Singlish. (4)
3. Singlish for something great, sure and not hollow. (6)
7. Mammal. (3)
11. Not positive. (2)
12. A river in the UK or a part of an engine. (3)
13. First name of crime fiction writer. (6)
14. Means nothing in Singlish. (7)
17. House for icy weather with a toilet in it. (5)
18. Singlish subjunctive. (3)
19. A variety of English. (8)
22. One who works a machine. (8)
24. Cause of trouble or misery in one's life. (4)
26. A system for paying income tax in instalments. (4)
27. Floor covering. (3)
28. A French cooking term for quick-frying. (5)
30. An abbreviation used to describe refined chemicals used in the laboratory. (2)
31. Discoverers. (7)
34. The army, navy and air force. (3)
36. An adjective in Singlish. (3)
38. Poem. (3)
39. Crippled. (4)

40. Closest. (7)
43. An ache in Singlish. (3)
44. Charged particle. (3)
45. Telephone girls' Singlish request. (4,2)
47. I, in Italy, opposite of a call in Singapore. (2)
49. A helper's job in the civil service. (2)
51. These days it is often a machine and not a person cleaning the roads. (6,7)
57. Singlish domestic. (4)

Down

1. Crabs in Singlish. (5)
2. Gaining knowledge. (8)
4. Sometimes the opposite of under. (2)
5. Large dwelling in Malaysian jungles. (4,5)
6. Contains a mistake or mistakes. (9)
7. Teenager's skin problem. (4)
8. Little boy at a wedding. (4,3)
9. A printer's measure. (2)
10. Surprising Chinese surname? (2)
15. Short Albert. (2)
16. Towards. (2)
20. Singapore is one. There are thousands in Indonesia. (6)
21. Terrible crime against the female sex. (4)
23. One who reduces the sail area on a Singlish watercourse. (6)
24. Singlish family members. (8)
25. Atmosphere surrounding a person or place. (4)
29. Singlish sound of an English exclamation? (5)
32. An element akin to chlorine and bromine. (6)
33. Boy who is a menace. (6)
34. Japanese surname of man who went to South Africa? (4)
35. The verb to be in the morning? (2)
37. Beautiful Malaysian beast. (5)

39. Institution of higher learning in London. (3)
41. You have to learn these when you get a new job. (5)
42. *The* in Spanish. (2)
46. A Singlish expression used when handing over an article? (2)
48. Be indebted to. (3)
50. Ladies should do this when shaking hands. (3)
52. Main Singapore entertainment. (2)
53. A hesitating Chinese surname? (2)
54. Disease that killed our forefathers but is now no longer a threat. (2)
55. A measure equal to one-sixth of an inch. (2)
56. Abbreviation for a well-known aesthetics institution in London. (2)

SOLUTION: Singlish Crossword 1

SINGLISH CROSSWORD 2

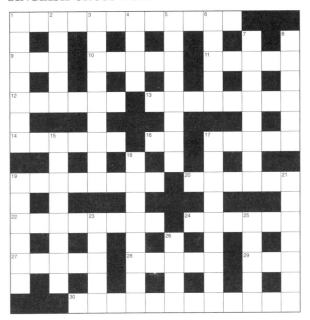

Cryptic Clues

Across

1. The pure oriental tint of the Singapore flag? (7,5)
9. Something strange in the old dodderer's head. (3)
10. Go in treating it as entertainment to begin with and ending as a consenter. (5)
11. Paradisiacal listlessness? (5)
12. Plea for Permanent Residency before a year is up? (6)
13. Singlish permit sought for absence from garden work. (8)
14. Terrible rain at the airport. (6)

16. A word with bisexual applications in Singlish. (2)
17. Malay name of a laser-sliced fish. (5)
19. Sounds more like the people's law than rustic beliefs. (8)
20. Positive points for electron flow. (6)
22. Singlish method of cost reduction. (8)
24. The she-fly turns to the pulpy part of fruits and vegetables. (6)
27. Perak, Singapore, Kinta, Muda are some names of this. (5)
28. Toss aside innovative thoughts? (5)
29. Ah! That sounds like really living for us. (3)
30. In early Singlish, a presumptive person was asked if these ancestors owned what they were abusing. (12)

Down

1. Hackin' at the composer in Singlish style. (7)
2. Asian country in need of aid? (5)
3. Basic mental confusion with a Mr Lee? (9)
4. Consuming cream teas. (4)
5. Fossilised in a nerd head. (8)
6. A Singlish disappearing act? Like smelly tea? (5)
7. Cooled in a controlled way, tempered and toughened, Anne takes the lead. (8)
8. Sounds like *to skin an animal* in Singlish or *steal a few*. (6)
15. A singular *30 Across* is an older one. (8)
17. A short game which is the target of the SDU. (6,3)
18. A tic in front causing chaffing. (8)
19. It starts with some ruffle and ends with some more confusion in the outburst of anger or admiration. (6)
21. Cunning Nye with one large and three small characters. (7)
23. The fault lies in the hearts of terrorists. (5)

25. A sudden rush to call a suit a suit in Singlish. (5)
26. Childish Singlish teats or stealers? (4)

Simple Clues

Across
1. A neutral paint colour used by oriental artists? (7,5)
9. Strange. (3)
10. Go in. (5)
11. Boredom or listlessness. (5)
12. Plea. (6)
13. Singlish Medical Certificate. (8)
14. Airport in Japan. (6)
16. A sexless word in Singlish. (2)
17. Malay name of a common fish. (5)
19. Traditional beliefs. (8)
20. Opposite of cathodes. (6)
22. To lay off staff in Singlish. (8)
24. Plumpy. (6)
27. Watercourse. (5)
28. Fresh thoughts. (5)
29. Present tense of verb to be with plural subject. (3)
30. Male ancestors. (12)

Down
1. Singlish pronunciation of the composer; 1810–49. (7)
2. Large Asian country. (5)
3. Basic; down to the fundamentals. (9)
4. Consumables. (4)
5. Stiffened. (8)
6. A Singlish mispronunciation of fooling someone. (5)
7. Changed metal crystalline structure by cooling. (8)
8. To steal little bits, or little bits at a time. (6)
15. A *farder* or a *marder* or a *brarder* is one. (8)

17. A short game which is the target of the SDU. (6,3)
18. The cause of slowing down machines and organisations. (8)
19. Uproar. (6)
21. Cunning. (7)
23. The fault lies in the hearts of terrorists. (5)
25. A digging tool in Singlish. (5)
26. Childish Singlish word for stealers? (4)

SOLUTION: Singlish Crossword 2

Y

Yohan The Singaporeans' lazy way of saying the name of the Japanese supermarket, Yaohan (Ya-o-han).

your *Your phone call* is heard very often. The English would say "There's a call for you." *Your phone call* would be used if a call had been booked or discussed previously.

R.K. Tongue describes *Your phone call* as substandard ESM (English of Singapore and Malaysia). We disagree with him and we raise this phrase as an example of borderline cases that will be debated and sorted out in due course. This book is probably full of such cases and we make no apology for nit-fine-screening our contents through a *Singlish-or-no* locally made mesh. In fact we hope criticism and argument will be stirred up. And hopefully (oops!) one goat will be sorted out from the *sheeps*; or whatever …

Z

zoning in … on the error-prone areas… In the teaching of pronunciation, the universal dilemma of deciding whether to zone in on the difficult areas or to cover the subject generally keeps coming up. Abercrombie is quoted on this in ref. 6, p. 145: "The learner instead of being taken systematically through each English vowel and consonant, and later, if there is time, through the complexities of intonation and rhythm, would have presented to him certain carefully chosen features on which to concentrate, the rest of his pronunciation being left to no more than a general supervision."

We end our nit-picking glossary of Singlish with a suggestion to Singaporean readers who feel they should break away from Singlish. It is inspired by a challenge to everyman made by Professor Dennis Enright, who during his stay in Singapore stirred many a Singapore undergrad into new sensitivities for the English language and pricked the sensitivities of some authorities. He said every man should write his own Faust book. Every Singaporean should compile his own Singlish tape; record the true Singlish word and follow it with the RP pronunciation.

There's a snag; you have to get the RP pronunciation right. And if you have nobody to ask you'll have to look up the dictionary. But you still have to get those key reference sounds right. We thought we could try to help. We made up a poem using the difficult reference words of the *Little Oxford English Dictionary* either as Singlish or as English. We tried but failed. We could not work in sing, cup, leg, poor, pin, or pen. See **rack**.

SHE HAD SUCH A BEAUTIFUL FACE

I met her at an eating place,
"Skew me. Can I share your taber?"
I yah-ed and went back to my book.
She had a lovely face.

"How can you eat and read!" she said.
"My mother weel never allourredit."
In silence I smiled into her eyes.
She blushed a beautiful red.
"Not only a boook bart a penceel too!
Do you always make marks in your book?"
I took in her body and smiled again.
I saw she had read my look.

"I suggest the prata and mutton curry."
"Again? Wazzat you sayed?"
"I suggest the prata and mutton curry."
"Bart it looks so hortt and raid.

"No. I tink I'll have the mee.
The keeng plawns look so beeg.
Haymee is my favourlite.
I'm a Hokkien dialect, you see."

When her food arrived she turned to me.
"I hate these plarsteek bowls."
"Yes," I agreed. "We shouldn't use them.
They cause those ozone holes."

"Hah," she replied.
And I sighed.
Her beautiful face was blank.
And only then did I realise,
that the bin beside us stank.

With a "Join me," she started to eat.
The soup dribbled down her chin;
splashed on her blouse all frilly with lace.
But she had such a beautiful face.

While smacking her lips she questioned me,
"Tell me, why do you read?"
At the innocence in her asking,
my heart began to bleed.

I told her of the wonder of words,
the musical ring of rhythmic beats.
I told her of William Blake,
and I told her of Shelley and Keats;
and of Shaw's wit,
and a little bit,
of the lilt of Longfellow's songs;
the Kipling thing of the Khyber pass,
and Whitman's lyrical *Leaves of Grass*.

I soared skylark-wild and free,
raved at the genius of Dylan T.,
told her of Yeats,
and H.E. Bates,
and T.S. Eliot's *Cats*.
Then switched to novels and horror;
Mary Shelley and vampire bats,
Sci. Fi. Clark and E.A. Poe,
Plots and intrigues of C.P. Snow.
And returned to the metered beat.
Lindsay lines that move your feet,
Sondheim songs that quicken the pulse,
making your bloodstream race.
Oh! She had such a beautiful face;
which was blank.
Then I noticed again,
that the litter-bin next to us stank.

We parted;
I, deflated;
She, unruffled,
cool as a cucumber.
But; I got her telephone number.

We met again.
Many times.
Burger King or Jack's Place,
Shenton or Toa Payoh.
She had such a beautiful face.

As the days flew,
our friendship grew.

Then suddenly,
one day,
she rang to say,
her folks were away,
would I like to come over to her place?
She had such a beautiful face.

I found the right block,
and the right floor hex,
and knocked on her door,
my thoughts in a turmoil of love and sex.

"Come in!
The lounge is so hortt.
The bedroom's air-con.
The lounge is nort."

She bade me sit beside her.
"Come seet beside me on the bade."
I sensed a seduction trap.
"Tarling, my hartt ees on fie-yer."
And then like a bolt from the blue,
she uttered, "Tarling, I luurve you."

I leapt from the bed, stricken with pain,
my stomach all twisted in knots,
ran in agony out of her flat,
and never ever saw her again.

I could take her unshaven armpits,
and the way she said her *thents*,
I could take her *howwerbourtits*,
and her clipped Singlish accents.
I coped with her *dis* and her *ders*,
and her mixing of *hees* and hers.
And over the months, I learnt to follow,
the l's for r's in her *tomollow*;
but, by the gods above,
her terrible mauling of *love*,
was more than my soul could swallow.

But she had such a beautiful face ...

References

1. Allen, C.A. *Tales from the South China Sea.* London: Andre Deutsch, 1983.
2. Boyd, L.M. *Boyd's Book of Odd Facts.* USA: Signet, 1980.
3. Burchfield, Robert. *The spoken word, A BBC Guide.* London: BBC, 1981.
4. Cohen, J.M. and M.J. *The Penguin Dictionary of Modern Quotations.* Second edition. London, 1980.
5. Crewe, W.J. *Singapore English and Standard English.* Singapore: Eastern Universities Press Sdn Bhd, 1977.
6. Foley, Joseph (editor). *New Englishes—The case for Singapore.* Singapore: Singapore University Press, 1988.
7. *Fowler's Modern English Usage.* Second edition revised by Sir Ernest Gowers. London: Oxford University Press, 1965.
8. Honey, John. *The Spoken Word.* London: Faber & Faber, 1989.
9. *It's a Fact!* London: Hamlyn Paperbacks, 1980.
10. Jones, Daniel. *English Pronouncing Dictionary.* 12th edition. London: The English Language Book Society, 1963.
11. Noss, R.B. (editor). *Varieties of English in South East Asia.* Singapore: Singapore University Press, 1983.

12. Oh Tiek Theam. *O-Pun Sesame*. Singapore: Eastern Universities Press Sdn Bhd, 1984.
13. *The Penguin Book of Comic and Curious Verse.*
14. Platt, John and Heidi Weber. *English in Singapore and Malaysia*. Kuala Lumpur: Oxford University Press, 1980.
15. Platt, John, Heidi Weber and Ho Mian Lian. 'Singapore and Malaysia', *Varieties of English around the world series*. Amsterdam/Philadelphia: John Benjamin Publishing Company, 1983.
16. *The Poetry of Singapore*. The Asean Committee on Culture and Information, 1985. Not for Sale.
17. *Quotations*. London: Bloomsbury Publishing Limited, Bookmart, 1990.
18. Toh Paik Choo. *Eh Goondu*. Singapore: Eastern Universities Press, 1982. Reissued by Times Books International, 1986.
19. Toh Paik Choo. *Friendship, Courtship, Hatred, Love*. Singapore: Times Books International, 1983.
20. Toh Paik Choo. *Lagi Goondu*. Singapore: Times Books International, 1986.
21. Tongue, R.K. *The English of Singapore and Malaysia.* Singapore: Eastern Universities Press, 1974, revised 1979.

The Authors

Rex Shelley is a businessman who has published books on the Japanese and three novels, two of which have won prizes. Born in Singapore in 1930, he lived in Malaysia for many years, and finished his education with a Chemistry degree from the University of Malaya and an Engineering-Economics degree from Cambridge, England.

He is a member of the Singapore Public Service Commission and Deputy Chairman of the Education Service Commission, but hastens to add that he has nothing to do with the teaching of English in those capacities.

He has never stopped playing the piano, keeps fit by swimming and is now on to painting on fabrics.

His co-authors, he says (and won't say anything more about them), are timorous friends cowering behind the apt *noms de plume* of Beng Kia-su and Takut bin Salah, which can both be translated freely as *'fraidie cats* or *mousies*.

A Letter to You, Reader

Skew me, please ahh ...
If you doan min' ...

We know dis is one good book but our auters also human lah. Sure got mistakes here an dere ... or maybe dey leff out some tings.

If you see cock-up or lobang, please write to Editor overall-in-charge one (address appended below) and give us feetback.

Also mabbie you got anarder one more better Singlish slang for telling. If you wan' we can mentioned you when we print again nextime, or when Lex Selly an his scrapegoats write followup (if dey still alive).

Send your letter to:
> Editor Overall-in-charge
> Times Editions
> Times Centre
> 1 New Industrial Road
> Singapore 1953

P.S. Please be inform, stamps for local now is 22 cents.